E-Participation in Southern Europe and the Balkans

The rapid development and the growing penetration of information and communication technologies (ICT) provide tremendous opportunities for a wide and cost effective application of the ideas of participative democracy and public participation in government decision and policy making. ICT can drive dramatic transformations in the quantity and quality of communication and interaction of government organizations with citizens, revitalizing and strengthening the modern representative democracy which currently faces big problems of reduced citizens' trust and involvement.

This book deals with the application of these e-participation ideas in the special and 'difficult', and at the same time highly interesting, national context of Southern Europe and the Balkans. The first chapter provides an overview of e-participation concepts and practices whilst the following chapters analyse pilot applications of e-participation concepts in eight different Southern European and Balkan countries (Spain, France, Italy, Slovenia, Serbia, Albania, Greece, Former Yugoslav Republic of Macedonia (FYROM)). They cover both the 'classical' e-participation paradigm, based on official e-participation spaces created, operated and controlled by government organizations as well as emerging new e-participation paradigms including e-participation based on web 2.0 social media, and 'scientific-level' e-participation, based on opening government data to the scientific community.

This book was originally published as a special issue of the *Journal of Balkan and Near Eastern Studies*.

Euripidis Loukis is Associate Professor of Information and Decision Support Systems at the University of Aegean, Greece, and also teaches at the National Academy of Public Administration. He has previously been Information Systems Advisor at the Ministry to the Presidency of Government, and Representative of Greece at the European Union in several e-government/e-participation committees.

Ann Macintosh is Professor of Digital Governance and Co-director of the Centre of Digital Citizenship at the University of Leeds, UK. She has acted as a specialist advisor for the OECD, the UN and the Commonwealth Secretariat. In 2009 she was awarded an Honorary Doctorate from Örebro University, Sweden, for recognition of her work in eParticipation.

Yannis Charalabidis is Assistant Professor of e-Governance Information Systems at the University of Aegean, Greece and also leads eGovernment & eBusiness Research in the Decision Support Systems Laboratory of National Technical University of Athens. In 2008 he received the Best Paper Award in the Electronic Government – Electronic Participation International Conference.

E-Participation in Southern Europe and the Balkans

Issues of Democracy and Participation Via Electronic Media

Edited by
**Euripidis Loukis, Ann Macintosh
and Yannis Charalabidis**

LONDON AND NEW YORK

First published 2013
by Routledge
2 Park Square, Milton Park, Abingdon, Oxon, OX14 4RN

Simultaneously published in the USA and Canada
by Routledge
711 Third Avenue, New York, NY 10017

First issued in paperback 2017

Routledge is an imprint of the Taylor & Francis Group, an informa business

© 2013 Taylor & Francis

This book is a reproduction of the *Journal of Balkan and Near Eastern Studies*, vol. 13, issue 1. The Publisher requests to those authors who may be citing this book to state, also, the bibliographical details of the special issue on which the book was based.

All rights reserved. No part of this book may be reprinted or reproduced or utilised in any form or by any electronic, mechanical, or other means, now known or hereafter invented, including photocopying and recording, or in any information storage or retrieval system, without permission in writing from the publishers.

Trademark notice: Product or corporate names may be trademarks or registered trademarks, and are used only for identification and explanation without intent to infringe.

British Library Cataloguing in Publication Data
A catalogue record for this book is available from the British Library

Typeset in Times New Roman
by Taylor & Francis Books

Publisher's Note
The publisher would like to make readers aware that the chapters in this book may be referred to as articles as they are identical to the articles published in the special issue. The publisher accepts responsibility for any inconsistencies that may have arisen in the course of preparing this volume for print.

ISBN 13: 978-1-138-10894-3 (pbk)
ISBN 13: 978-0-415-62359-9 (hbk)

Contents

1. Introduction
   Euripidis Loukis, Ann Macintosh and Yannis Charalabidis   1

2. Using advanced information technologies for increasing public participation in the Greek Parliament
   Euripidis Loukis   13

3. Electronic participation pilots in the Western Balkans: lessons from the field
   Sotirios Koussouris, Yannis Charalabidis, Loukas Kipenis, Dimitrios Askounis and Odetta Stavri   37

4. Constructing and implementing e-participation tools in the Emilia Romagna Region: assemblages and sense-making
   Andrea Resca   59

5. Learning from eParticipation initiatives of regional and local level authorities in Greece and Spain
   Eleni Panopoulou, Efthimios Tambouris, Elena Sanchez-Nielsen, Maria Zotou and Konstantinos Tarabanis   77

6. Using participative GIS and e-tools for involving citizens of Marmo Platano–Melandro area in European programming activities
   Beniamino Murgante, Lucia Tilio, Viviana Lanza and Francesco Scorza   97

7. Participatory policy process design: lessons learned from three European regions
   Clelia Colombo, Mateja Kunstelj, Francesco Molinari and Ljupco Todorovski   117

   Index   139

Introduction

EURIPIDIS LOUKIS, ANN MACINTOSH and YANNIS CHARALABIDIS

There has been a growing interest of public sector researchers and practitioners in the last 25 years in the involvement of citizens in government decision-making and policy development. This is seen as a complement and reinforcement of representative democracy where citizens not only elect their representatives, who take responsibility for government decisions and policies, but also provide their feedback to them on a continuous and systematic basis. A sound theoretical foundation for these ideas has been developed, which has been followed by practical application in many countries all over the world. Barber (1984)[1] introduces the concept of 'strong democracy', which is characterized by active citizen participation and discussion among opposing views. However, he argues that this is not easy, since 'it entails listening no less than speaking, it is affective as well as cognitive ...', and also requires sufficient 'civic education', which can strengthen public discourse and participation in the democratic process. He proposes three forms of civic education for this purpose: formal education in citizenship (including teaching on a nation's constitution, legal system and political practice), private sphere social activity focusing on debate about its effect on local issues and participatory politics itself, which he argues is the most successful form of civic education. In the same direction Held (1987),[2] combining work of previous researchers, defines an emergent new model of democracy, which he termed as 'participatory democracy'. A key principle of this model is that:

> the equal right to self-development can only be achieved in a participatory society, a society which fosters a sense of political efficacy, nurtures a concern for collective problems and contributes to the formation of a knowledgeable citizenry capable of taking a sustained interest in the governing process.

In a subsequent work Held (1996)[3] distinguishes nine different models of democracy; one of them is the participatory model, which reflects the need to engage both citizens and civil society organizations in the policy-making process. However, he emphasizes that in order to achieve this it is important that citizens are sufficiently informed and active. Fishkin (1997)[4] criticizes political opinion surveys that force people to judge instantly issues on which they may have no opinion or have given little thought, and proposes 'mass' deliberation by citizens instead,

---

[1] B. Barber, *Strong Democracy: Participatory Politics for a New Age*, University of California Press, Berkeley, CA, 1984.

[2] D. Held, *Models of Participation*, Polity Press, Cambridge, 1987.

[3] D. Held, *Models of Democracy*, Blackwell, Cambridge, 1996.

[4] J. S. Fishkin, *The Voice of the People—Public Opinion and Democracy*, Yale University Press, New Haven, CT and London, 1997.

which should complement 'elite' deliberation by elected representatives. He states that 'A major part of the problem of democratic reform is how to promote mass deliberation—how to bring people into the process under conditions where they can be engaged to think seriously and fully about public issues.'

Another research stream focuses on understanding the nature of public policy problems and the methodology of finding solutions for them, and concludes that they gradually become less well defined and more complex, and for this reason extensive public participation is required for defining and solving them. Rittel and Weber (1973)[5] argue that previously public policy problems, though they were not trivial, had a clear and widely accepted definition and objectives, and could be solved mainly by experts using 'first generation' methods; these methods are based on mathematical optimization algorithms and focus on achieving some predefined objectives with the lowest possible resources. However, this situation has changed dramatically and public policy problems tend to become 'wicked': they do not have a clear and widely agreed definition and objectives, and are characterized by high complexity and many stakeholders with different and heterogeneous problem views, values and concerns. This new generation of problems cannot be solved with the above 'technocratic' first generation methods, and require a different 'second generation' approach, which should combine public participation and technocratic analysis. In particular, the first and fundamental step for addressing them is consultation and argumentation among problem stakeholders, which includes discourse, reasoning, arguments and negotiation taking place, aiming to synthesize different views and formulate a shared definition of the problem, the objectives to be achieved and the existing alternative solutions. Having this as a base it is possible then in a second step to proceed to a technocratic analysis performed by experts using mathematical optimization algorithms for solving the problem that has been defined in the first step. Subsequent research on such problems has revealed that the above participative/argumentative approach to addressing them can be greatly supported by 'Issue Based Information Systems' (IBIS),[6] which support structured deliberation among the stakeholders of the problem.

Based on the above theoretical foundations the concept of public participation has been gradually formulated. The OECD[7] defines public participation as a combination of three main activities: provision of information by the government to the citizens concerning future public policies under development, consultation on them with the citizens and also support of citizens' active participation and initiatives (such as the suggestion of new policy options or discussion topics in addition to the ones proposed by government). Rowe and Frewer (2004)[8] define public participation as 'the practice of consulting and involving members of the

---

[5] H. W. J. Rittel and M. M. Weber, 'Dilemmas in a general theory of planning', *Policy Sciences*, 4, 1973, pp. 155–169.

[6] W. Kunz and H. Rittel, 'Issues as elements of information systems', Working Paper No. 131, University of California, Berkeley, 1979; J. Conklin and M. Begeman, 'gIBIS: a tool for all reasons', *Journal of the American Society for Information Science*, 40(3), 1989, pp. 200–213; J. Conklin, 'Dialog mapping: reflections on an industrial strength case study', in P. Kirschner, S. Buckingham Shum and C. Carr (eds), *Visualizing Argumentation: Software Tools for Collaborative and Educational Sense-Making*, Springer-Verlag, London, 2003.

[7] OECD (Organization for Economic Co-operation & Development), *Engaging Citizens in Policy-Making: Information, Consultation and Public Participation*, PUMA Policy Brief, Paris, 2001.

[8] G. Rowe and L. J. Frewer, 'Evaluating public-participation exercises: a research agenda', *Science, Technology & Human Values*, 29(4), 2004, pp. 512–557.

public in the agenda-setting, decision-making and policy forming activities of organizations or institutions responsible for policy development'. They view it as a move away from an 'elitist model', in which public sector managers and experts are the basic source of public policies, to a new model, in which citizens have a more active role and voice. However, it is made clear that the objective of such a participatory democracy is not to replace representative democracy and establish a new order, but to improve and strengthen it, and contribute to overcoming the existing 'democratic deficits' and the growing abstention and disengagement of citizens from politics.

Governments of many countries have made considerable efforts in order to apply the above ideas,[9] promote public participation and strengthen their relations with their citizens. In particular governments initiate and support the above-mentioned three types of interactions with their citizens in various stages of the public policy-making cycle (starting from the agenda setting stage up to the monitoring and evaluation stage):

(I) Information provision: a 'one-way relation', in which government produces and delivers information to be used by citizens (it includes both 'active' information initiated by government and 'passive' as a response to citizens' demands).
(II) Consultation: an asymmetric 'two-way relation', in which citizens provide views and feedback to government on issues and questions that government has previously defined.
(III) Active participation: a more symmetric 'two-way relation' between government and citizens, in which citizens have a wider role in proposing new policy options and discussion topics, in addition to the ones proposed by government, and in shaping the policy dialogue in general, though the government still has the responsibility for the final decisions.

The main objectives that governments have in initiating and supporting these three types of interactions are:

- improving the quality of public policies, by taking advantage of valuable policy-relevant sources of information, knowledge and also perspectives and viewpoints that exist in the society,
- responding to the expectations of citizens that their voices should be heard and their views should be seriously considered in public decision and policy-making by all levels of government,

---

[9] OECD, *Citizens as Partners—Information, Consultation and Public Participation in Policy-Making*, OECD Publication Service, Paris, 2001; OECD, *Engaging Citizens in Policy-Making*, op. cit.; OECD, *Evaluating Public Participation in Policy Making*, OECD Publication Service, Paris, 2004; G. G. Curtis, 'Issues and challenges—global e-government/e-participation models, measurement and methodology—a framework for moving forward', *Workshop on E-Participation and E-Government: Understanding the Present and Creating the Future*, Budapest, Hungary, 2006; Commission of the European Communities, 'i2010 eGovernment Action Plan: accelerating eGovernment in Europe for the benefit of all', *Communication from the Commission to the Council*, COM (2006) 173, European Parliament, European Economic and Social Committee and the Committee of the Regions, Brussels, 25 April 2006; P. Timmers, *Agenda for eDemocracy—An EU Perspective*, European Commission, Brussels, 2007; United Nations, 'United Nations e-Government Survey 2008—from e-Government to connected Governance', Department of Economic and Social Affairs, Division for Public Administration and Development Management, New York, 2008.

- responding to calls for greater government transparency and accountability,
- strengthening public trust in government and reversing the declining confidence in politics and key public institutions.

For achieving these objectives governments use several 'offline' methods designed to inform, consult and involve those affected by particular decisions and public policies;[10] the most widely used of them are public hearings/inquiries, public opinion surveys, citizens' juries/panels, focus groups, citizen/public advisory committees, consensus conferences, negotiated rule-making and referenda.

The rapid development and the growing penetration of information and communication technology (ICT), and especially the Internet, provide tremendous opportunities for a wide and cost effective application of the above ideas. ICT can drive significant transformations in the quantity and quality of communication and interaction of government agencies with citizens. This enables government agencies to gain a better and deeper understanding of the problems, needs, concerns and values of groups of citizens and in general the societies they are serving, and therefore make in a timely fashion the required decisions, public policies, programmes and legislations. These capabilities resulted in the emergence and gradual development of electronic participation (or e-participation). Saebo et al. (2008)[11] define it as the extension and transformation of participation in societal democratic and consultative processes through the exploitation of ICT. The OECD[12] provide a more detailed definition of e-participation as the use of ICTs for supporting the provision of information to citizens concerning government activities and public policies, the consultation on them with the citizens and also their active participation in all the stages of the policy-making life cycle: agenda setting, policy analysis, policy formulation, policy implementation and policy monitoring/evaluation. Macintosh and Whyte (2006)[13] suggest that e-participation concerns the use of ICT for supporting not only the 'top-down' engagement of citizens, for example, via initiatives promoted by the government, but also 'ground-up' efforts as well, in which citizens, organizations of civil society and other democratically established groups convey their needs and opinions to elected representatives and government.

ICTs offer unprecedented huge capabilities for increasing citizens' access to government information, promoting transparency, accountability and fighting corruption. They enable governments to make available through the Internet large amounts of information concerning their activities, decisions, spending and financial situation in general, and policy white papers; furthermore, they provide citizens with powerful tools for searching, selecting and integrating the large amounts of government information, in order to satisfy their particular information needs and interests. However, this poses several challenges. Highly important is not only the quantity of government information provided online to

---

[10] G. Rowe and L. J. Frewer, 'Public participation methods: a framework for evaluation', *Science, Technology & Human Values*, 25(1), 2000, pp. 3–29.

[11] Saebo, J. Rose and L. S. Flak, 'The shape of eParticipation: characterizing an emerging research area', *Government Information Quarterly*, 25, 2008, pp. 400–428.

[12] OECD, *Engaging Citizens Online for Better Policy-Making*, OECD Observer Policy Brief, Paris, 2003; OECD, *Promise and Problems of e-Democracy: Challenges of Online Citizen Engagement*, OECD Publication Service, Paris, 2004.

[13] A. Macintosh and A. Whyte, 'Towards an evaluation framework for eParticipation', *Transforming Government: People, Process & Policy*, 2(1), 2008, pp. 16–30.

citizens, but also its quality as well, in terms of its accessibility, relevance and utility to citizens wishing to be informed and participate in policy-making. The design of electronic provision of government information should start from the perspective of the end-users of it, and should be based on an assessment of their needs and their capacity to find, understand and use this information. Enhancing the accessibility of online information can be achieved by various means, such as organization of online information in terms of specific life events or policy issues and provision of search engines, online glossaries (explaining basic legal and technocratic terms used in government documents), multilingual translations of government documents and software tools making them more intelligible (such as visualizations of the main points of major documents in a simple schematic manner,[14] which can be understood by a much wider mass of citizens than the initial documents). If the above challenges are not effectively addressed, then the benefits of online government information provision will be much lower than its real potential, and mainly limited to some highly educated and knowledgeable groups of society.

Furthermore, the huge interactivity capabilities offered by modern ICTs has the potential to expand the scope, breadth and depth of government consultations with citizens and other stakeholders on key government policies and decisions. Many ICT tools have been developed and are available to governments for collecting citizens' views and suggestions on important issues, such as government consultation spaces, e-mail lists, online discussion forums, online mediation systems for supporting deliberation and also various means of ICT support of 'traditional' consultations. Additionally, there are advanced ICT tools for increasing the quality of the government–citizens interaction by enabling more structured and focused e-consultations.[15] However, there are many challenges that should be addressed in order to exploit this huge potential. The e-consultations usually produce large amounts of citizens' postings, which include useful input, views and knowledge, so they have to be analysed, exploited and integrated in the policy-making process; also feedback has to be provided to citizens on how their comments and suggestions have been used for reaching decisions or policy proposals. Therefore, it is necessary to develop appropriate processes and ICT tools for these purposes. Another issue is 'self-selection' of the participants in these e-consultations, among those who already have access to ICTs, raising the risk of over-representation of a small cross section of the population and the resulting increase of the already existing

---

[14] A. Renton and A. Macintosh, 'Computer supported argument maps as a policy memory', *Information Society Journal*, 23(2), 2007, pp. 125–133; E. Loukis, A. Xenakis and N. Tserpeli, 'Using argument visualization to enhance e-Participation in the legislation formation process', *IFIP First International Conference on e-Participation—ePart 2009*, Linz, Austria, September 2009; A. Macintosh, T. F. Gordon and A. Renton, 'Providing argument support for eParticipation', *Journal of Information, Technology & Politics (JITP)*, 6(1), 2009, pp. 43–59.

[15] T. F. Gordon and N. Karacapilidis, 'The Zeno argumentation framework', paper presented at the Sixth International Conference on Artificial Intelligence and Law (ICAIL '97), 1997; N. Karacapilidis, E. Loukis and S. Dimopoulos, 'Computer-supported G2G collaboration for public policy and decision making', *Journal of Enterprise Information Management*, 18(5), 2005, pp. 602–624; A. Xenakis and E. Loukis, 'An investigation of the use of structured e-Forum for enhancing e-Participation in parliaments', *International Journal of Electronic Governance*, 3(2), 2010, pp. 134–147.

'digital divide'.[16] This term is increasingly used in the last decade to denote that despite the increasing penetration of ICT, and especially the Internet, in large parts of the populations of many countries (mainly of high or medium economic development), there are still considerable groups (e.g. citizens of low income, low education or old age) without access to ICTs and/or without sufficient skills to use them; this is increasing their exclusion from the highly ICT-dependent modern economy and society, so it might increase the already existing social inequalities. However, such risks can be reduced by serious government efforts to enable wider access to ICT by citizens who cannot afford it (e.g. community centres, public kiosks, etc.), and also adequate promoting and supporting e-consultations, so that there is wide participation in them of citizens from various social groups. Another question is what will be the impact of e-participation on the role of the traditional mediators of citizens' voice (e.g. elected representatives, civil society organizations, etc.)? Are we going to have similar phenomena with the ones observed in the e-business world[17] (removal or reduction of power and role of many existing commercial intermediaries between producers and consumers, and at the same time emergence of new ICT-based intermediaries)?

Finally, ICT can also support and facilitate a more active participation of citizens, through online tools and discussion formats which enable them to set the agenda for discussion (e.g. raise new issues that have to be discussed, in addition to the ones raised by the government), submit their own proposals and policy options and in general shape the final outcomes. This dimension of e-participation is the least explored, with only some types of ICT tools having been investigated for this purpose, such as e-petition spaces[18] (in which citizens can enter petitions to the government or parliament, and solicit support and signatures), electronic discussion groups supporting the development of new policy options and the deliberation on them and online referenda. The main barriers to the wider use of these more active and innovative forms of e-participation are not technical, but mainly cultural, associated with government's resistance to these new forms of partnership with citizens and civil society in policy-making.

The high potential of ICT in supporting, facilitating and enhancing the above three dimensions of public participation has led, on the one hand, to a first application of these ideas in many countries (mainly electronic information provision, much less electronic consultation and to a limited extent ICT support for active participation).[19] On the other hand, it has led to the emergence of a

---

[16] OECD, *Learning to Bridge the Digital Divide*, OECD Publication Service, Paris, 2000; P. Norris, *Digital Divide: Civic Engagement, Information Poverty, and the Internet Worldwide*, Cambridge University Press, New York, 2001; K. Mossberger, C. J. Tolbert and M. Stansbury, *Virtual Inequality: Beyond the Digital Divide*, Georgetown University Press, Washington, DC, 2003.

[17] T. Jelassi and A. Enders, *Strategies for E-Business: Concepts and Cases*, FT Prentice Hall, London, 2008; D. Chaffey, *E-Business and E-Commerce Management: Strategy, Implementation and Practice*, FT Prentice Hall, London, 2009.

[18] D. Santucci, 'Studying e-petitions: state of the art and challenges', *ESF-LIU Conference on Electronic Democracy*, Vadstena, Sweden, 2007; P. Cruickshank, N. Edelmann and C. Smith, 'Signing an e-Petition as a transition from lurking to participation', in E. Tambouris, A. Macintosh and O. Glassey (eds), *Second IFIP International Conference on Electronic Participation—ePart 2010*, Lausanne, Switzerland, 2010.

[19] J. Hoff, K. Lofgren and L. Torpe, 'The state we are in: e-democracy in Denmark', *Information Polity*, 8, 2003, pp. 49–66; D. F. Norris, 'E-Democracy and E-Participation among local governments in

lively e-participation research area,[20] which investigates the use of various types of ICT for public participation purposes, the extent of exploitation of the above potential of ICT, the benefits and in general the value they generate, and the impact on political processes and on society in general, the effects of various contextual factors, the critical success factors and also the above-mentioned challenges that e-participation poses. Furthermore, recently it has started dealing with the exploitation of the emerging Web 2.0 social media, which have already attracted large numbers of users, for extending public participation.[21] The e-participation research area is by nature interdisciplinary, combining elements from the technological, political, social and administrative sciences.

This Special Issue aims to contribute to the investigation of the above research questions in a very special national context, the one of the Southern European and Balkan countries. The Balkan countries are characterized as 'semi-periphery' or 'late development' ones,[22] as on the one hand they are part of the economically developed world, but on the other they did not directly participate in the big transformations that took place in Western Europe and led to the development of the industrial capitalism and the concomitant political institutions and culture. These big economic and political transformations were 'imported' later in the Balkans from the 'early development' countries of Western Europe, and were greatly shaped by and combined with local institutions and practices. Later these countries lived for a long time under communist regimes, and their return to a market economy and representative democracy was followed by an outbreak of conflicts among ethnic groups, or even violence in the case of former Yugoslavia which led to its disintegration. All these resulted in underdeveloped democratic institutions and culture in the Balkan countries. However, the state in the Balkan countries, despite its democratic deficits, had traditionally a dominant role in the economic activity and development. The Southern European countries (Greece, Portugal, Italy and Spain) are characterized by some distinct specificities and differences from the Northern (Scandinavian) and West European ones with respect to the role and the basic characteristics of the state.[23] In Southern Europe

---

Footnote 19 continued
the U.S.', *Symposium on E-Participation and Local Democracy*, 2006; R. Medaglia, 'Measuring the diffusion of eParticipation: a survey on Italian local government', *Information Polity*, 12, 2007, pp. 265–280; United Nations, op. cit.

[20] J. Rose and C. Sanford, 'Mapping eParticipation research: four central challenges', *Communications of the Association for Information Systems*, 20, 2007, pp. 909–943; Saebo *et al.*, op. cit.; A. Macintosh, S. Coleman and A. Schneeberger, 'eParticipation: the research gaps', in A. Macintosh and E. Tambouris (eds), *Electronic Participation: Proceedings of First International Conference—ePart 2009*, LNCS 5694, 2009, pp. 1–11.

[21] Y. Punie, G. Misuraca and D. Osimo, 'Public Services 2.0: the impact of social computing on public services', *JRC Scientific and Technical Reports*, European Commission, Joint Research Centre–Institute for Prospective Technological Studies, 2009; Y. Charalabidis, G. Gionis and E. Loukis, 'Policy processes support through interoperability with social media', *5th Mediterranean Conference on Information Systems 2010 (MCIS 2010)*, Haifa, Israel, 25–27 September 2010; Y. Charalabidis, G. Gionis, E. Ferró and E. Loukis, 'Towards a systematic exploitation of Web 2.0 and simulation modeling tools in public policy process', *IFIP Second International Conference on e-Participation—ePart 2010*, Lausanne, Switzerland, 29 August–2 September 2010.

[22] N. Mouzelis, *Modern Greece: Facets of Underdevelopment*, Macmillan Press, London, 1978; N. Mouzelis, *Politics in the Semi-periphery: Early Parliamentarism and Late Industrialization in the Balkans and Latin America*, Macmillan Press, London, 1986; N. Mouzelis, *From Reform to Modernization*, Themelio, Athens, 2002.

[23] J. M. Maravall, 'Politics and policy: economic reforms in Southern Europe', in L. C. Bresser

the state has 'assisted' the development of capitalism to a much greater extent than in Northern and Western Europe, resulting in the establishment of an 'assisted capitalism' which is contrasted to 'competitive capitalism'. The role of the state in South Europe includes ownership of important corporations, protectionism and patronage of certain industrial sectors and social groups. As a result many groups became accustomed to depending on the state for their wealth and power (e.g. businesses relying on the state for loans and contracts, public sector employees relying on the state for obtaining much better social insurance, health and pension schemes than private sector employees). At the same time all the above-mentioned Southern European countries experienced dictatorship periods during the 20th century, which undermined democratic institutions and culture. The above history has resulted in some distinct characteristics of the state as to its relation with society: political clientelism 'at the top' (extensive politicization of the higher civil service) and 'at the bottom' (parties offering to their voters jobs in the public sector), uneven distribution of public servants (as another form of clientelism 'at the bottom': some highly desirable public services offering very good employment terms were overstaffed, while some others, though critical for society but not much desirable, were understaffed), excessive legalism and formalism (overproduction of laws, decrees and regulations resulting in high inflexibility and at the same time informal arrangements) and lack of administrative elite (with the exception of Spain).

It is therefore quite interesting to examine the interaction between the emerging e-participation ideas and this special national context, and gain an understanding of how e-participation is shaped by this context and at the same time what impact it can have on this context. In this direction the Special Issue includes six papers, which describe and analyse pilot applications of these e-participation ideas in seven Southern European and Balkan countries (Spain, France, Italy, Serbia, Albania, Greece, Yugoslav Republic of Macedonia (FYROM)) using a variety of approaches (both qualitative and quantitative ones). The first paper entitled 'Using Advanced Information Technologies for Increasing Public Participation in the Greek Parliament' by Euripidis Loukis describes and evaluates a first attempt of the Greek Parliament to use two advanced ICTs, computer supported arguments visualization and structured e-forum, for increasing the quantity and quality of public participation in the legislation formation process. From the quantitative and qualitative multi-perspective evaluation it has been concluded that using visualizations of the main parliamentary documents can make them more understandable by the citizens, contributing to a wider dissemination and discussion of them and promoting transparency and accountability. With respect to the use of structured e-forum it has been concluded that it can enhance the quality and focus of the e-consultations on legislation under formation, promoting interaction with the society and accessibility. However, the structure it imposes necessitates high mental effort from the participants, and this might make it less suitable for and usable by lower

---

Footnote 23 continued
Pereira, J. M. Maravall and A. Przeworski (eds), *Economic Reforms in New Democracies: A Social Democratic Approach*, Cambridge University Press, Cambridge, 1993, pp. 77–131; G. Pagoulatos, 'Financial interventionism and liberalization in Southern Europe: state, bankers, and the politics of disinflation', *Journal of Public Policy*, 23(2), 2003, pp. 171–199; D. A. Sotiropoulos, 'Southern European public bureaucracies in comparative perspective', *West European Politics*, 27(3), 2004, pp. 405–422.

education groups of the society, limiting the above benefits to the higher education groups and contributing to an increase of the existing 'digital divide'.

The second paper entitled 'Electronic Participation Pilots in the Western Balkans: Lessons from the Field' by Sotirios Koussouris, Yannis Charalabidis, Loukas Kipenis, Dimitrios Askounis and Odetta Stavri describes and evaluates a series of successful e-participation pilots in the Western Balkans (Albania, FYROM and Serbia), an area with intensive national and international tensions and conflicts, and rather young and immature democratic institutions. The pilots are conducted using an Internet-based ICT platform which allows citizens to comment and discuss the news items as they appear on the news agencies' websites. The conclusions of the evaluation of the usability and political usefulness of this ICT platform were in general positive, and this advocates the potential of e-participation ICT in such special and highly difficult contexts (with tensions, lack of trust, immature democratic institutions, etc.). The participants felt that such e-participation systems might have a positive impact on the local political life, and contribute to highlighting and addressing certain political issues, and also to the improvement of cooperation between NGOs, governmental organizations, news agencies and parliaments, and in general to bridging the existing gaps between citizens and governments. However, the existing tensions between the above countries had a negative impact on the cross-country e-consultation attempts.

The third paper entitled 'Constructing and Implementing e-Participation Tools in the Emilia Romagna Region: Assemblages and Sense-Making' by Andrea Resca presents a study of an e-participation project led by the Emilia Romagna Region, Italy, in collaboration with other Italian public administrations. Initially the involved public administrations put in collaboration together already existing technological artefacts that each of them had developed previously and composed an ad hoc technological solution for supporting e-consultations, which was then used for two e-consultations on two controversial issues of the Municipality of Modena. This 'assemblage' is examined from three perspectives: technical compatibility, functional compatibility and institutional compatibility, and the main problems/issues identified in the first two perspectives are discussed. The analysis of these two e-consultations shows that though the numbers of participants and postings was lower than expectations (indicating that the use of 'social brokers' for attracting more participants would be useful) the discussion was fruitful, new ideas emerged and inputs from participants led to interventions that were effectively put into practice; also hostile attitudes that existed gradually vanished.

The fourth paper is entitled 'Learning from e-Participation Initiatives of Regional and Local Level Authorities in Greece and Spain' and has been authored by Eleni Panopoulou, Efthimios Tambouris, Elena Sanchez-Nielsen, Maria Zotou and Konstantinos Tarabanis. It examines and compares the e-participation capabilities offered by the official websites of regional authorities of Greece and Spain, and also success stories of e-participation at the city level. It concludes that although e-participation is a political priority at the EU level, it is not yet adequately advanced in the regional and local authorities of these two countries. Spain scores good in electronic information provision and average in e-consultation, while Greece scores average in both; however, ICT-supported active participation measures are very low in both countries.

The fifth paper is entitled 'Using Participative GIS and e-Tools for Involving Citizens of Marmo Platano–Melandro Area in European Programming Activities' and has been authored by Beniamino Murgante, Lucia Tilio, Viviana Lanza and Francesco Scorza. It presents and analyses an e-participation pilot using Web 2.0 tools (such as blogs) and geographical information systems (GIS) in Marmo Platano–Melandro, Italy, aiming at the collaborative elaboration of a local development programme. This Internet-based approach shows a high potential to provide effective means through which planners can fully engage with the communities they serve through a more informed and 'bottom-up' planning process. However, the authors remark that such bottom-up participative local development planning processes are an exception in current practices, due to a lack of such a culture in most local governments, so too many resources are devoted to manage administrative procedures rather than to develop effective planning.

The final paper is 'Participatory Policy Process Design: Lessons Learned from Three European Regions' by Clelia Colombo, Mateja Kunstelj, Francesco Molinari and Ljupčo Todorovski, and focuses on the organization of e-participation. It presents a participatory workflow model, providing useful guidance for connecting various regional offline participation and e-participation sessions, and for integrating them in the policy-design process at the EU level. The paper assesses the benefits of implementing the proposed workflow in three South European regions (Catalonia, Spain; Toscana, Italy; and Poitou-Charentes, France), presents the lessons learned and discusses its potential. It is concluded that ICTs have a big potential for supporting citizen participation in public decision-making, although their effectiveness in participatory processes is highly related to the design and implementation of the whole project and the political will. Also, it is of critical importance to sustain coherence between the various offline participation processes (taking place in different locations and times) and the corresponding virtual debates on the same topic; an electronic debate platform could be used for this purpose, enabling previous debates to be maintained online, detect the main opinions, standpoints and arguments among participants and publicize documents of interest for the participatory process.

The papers of this Special Issue provide evidence that ICT, and especially the Internet, can be a very useful tool for increasing the quantity (more participating citizens) and the quality (better, more substantial and deliberative political discussions) of public participation in various government decisions and policies (such as legislation formulation, regional development planning, city regulations, etc.) in the national contexts of the Southern European and Balkan countries. These national contexts are characterized by a highly important and strong role of the state in the economic and social development on the one hand, and at the same time deficiencies in its communication with and control by the society on the other, due to weaknesses of the democratic institutions and culture (more in the Balkan countries and less in the Southern European ones). The findings of the above papers, though they are based on pilot and small-scale e-participation applications, indicate that ICTs have the potential to contribute to closing this gap and increase the transparency of government and its interaction with society; the asynchronous and remote non-face-to-face communication capabilities offered by modern ICT can enable a more calm, thoughtful and argumentative political dialogue even in very difficult situations characterized by lack of trust, negative feelings and hostility. However, this is not going to be an easy task, as there are many preconditions for this, such as appropriate ICT tools that can be used even by citizens of low education and ICT skills (while highly complex ones might finally result in increasing the 'digital divide'), overcoming cultural resistances from government employees (who are not accustomed to such intensive interaction with society) and using appropriate promotion and 'social brokers' for attracting participants. Also, in some difficult cases with a lot of conflict among opposing social or/and ethnic groups it might be necessary initially to take some trust building actions, before starting even an electronic discussion among them. Finally, it should be emphasized that governments in this area are currently exploiting the potential of e-participation only to a limited extent (using ICT mainly for information provision, but less for consultation and much less for supporting more active forms of citizens' participation), so it is necessary to experiment more with these advanced forms of e-participation as well.

Euripidis Loukis is Assistant Professor of Information and Decision Support Systems at the University of the Aegean, Greece. Also, he is teaching e-Government at the National Academy of Public Administration. Formerly he has been Information Systems Advisor at the Ministry to the Presidency of Government, Technical Director of the 'Program for the Modernization of Greek Public Administration' of the Second European Union Support Framework and Representative of Greece at the Management Committees of the Programs IDA ('Interchange of Data between Administrations') and 'Telematics for Administration' of the European Union.

Ann Macintosh is Professor of Digital Governance and Co-director of the Centre of Digital Citizenship at the University of Leeds, UK. Her work in digital governance is both applied and conceptual; the aim is not simply to design applications using new media, but to understand the changing nature of citizenship and governance in a networked society. She has acted as a specialist advisor for the OECD, the UN and the Commonwealth Secretariat. In 2009 she was awarded an Honorary Doctorate from Örebro University, Sweden for recognition of her work in eParticipation, in particular the interplay between humans, technology and governance.

Yannis Charalabidis is Assistant Professor of e-Governance Information Systems at the University of the Aegean, Greece. He teaches Government Service Systems, Enterprise Interoperability, Government Transformation and Citizen Participation both in the University of the Aegean and in the National Technical University of Athens. Previously he has been employed for several years as an Executive Director in Singular IT Group, leading software development and company expansion in Europe, India and the USA. He has also been the Coordinator or Technical Leader in numerous FP6, FP7 and National research projects in the areas of e-Business and e-Governance.

Using advanced information technologies for increasing public participation in the Greek Parliament

EURIPIDIS LOUKIS

Introduction

Parliaments are institutions of vital importance for modern democracies with highly important responsibilities: making laws, communicating with and representing citizens and overseeing the executive. The rapid growth and penetration of information and communication technologies (ICTs) has changed considerably the environment in which parliaments operate: citizens (and especially the youth), firms and government agencies are increasingly using ICT both for doing their internal work more efficiently and for communicating with others. Responding to this trend, in combination with the highly information-intensive nature of their responsibilities and tasks, parliaments have started using ICTs for supporting both their internal operations (e.g. for managing their numerous legislative documents, for financial accounting, etc.) and their communication with citizens and groups interested in the legislation under formation and discussion. According to the *World e-Parliament Report 2010*[1] of the 'Global Centre for ICT in Parliament' (a partnership initiative of the United Nations[2] and the Inter-Parliamentary Union)[3] there is a growing use of ICTs by parliaments all over the world driven by their fundamental values and objectives: representativeness, transparency, accessibility, accountability and effectiveness.[4] In particular, the study presented in the above report, which has been based on a survey of 134 parliaments from all over the world, concludes that there is wide use of 'basic' ICT tools by them. For instance, almost all the surveyed parliaments have a website (for promoting transparency and accountability), 96 per cent have a local area network (LAN) (for increasing effectiveness), 80 per cent provide Members of Parliament (MPs) with either desktop or laptop computers (also for increasing effectiveness), while 78 per cent reported that most or some MPs use e-mail in order to communicate with citizens (for promoting accessibility, interaction with society and representativeness). However, the same study also concludes that there is much lower use of more advanced ICT with high potential to be very useful to parliaments for achieving their objectives and promoting their values. For instance, less than half of the

---

[1] *World e-Parliament Report 2010*, Global Centre for ICT in Parliament, United Nations and Inter-Parliamentary Union, 2010, available at: <www.ictparliament.org>.
[2] <www.un.org>.
[3] <www.ictparliament.org>.
[4] *Parliament and Democracy in the Twenty-First Century: A Guide to Good Practice*, Inter-Parliamentary Union, Geneva, 2006.

surveyed parliaments have systems supporting the management of proposed legislation documents all over their life cycle (which would considerably increase internal effectiveness and transparency), only 25 per cent use the XML standard for parliamentary documents (which would improve processing and dissemination capabilities, promoting effectiveness, accessibility and transparency), while much less, only 16 per cent, organize e-consultations on bills (which would considerably enhance accessibility, interaction with society and representativeness).

It is therefore of critical importance for parliaments to go beyond the basic ICT, and select, assess and use appropriate more advanced ICT in order to achieve to a higher extent their above-mentioned objectives. Due to the information-intensive nature of their tasks this is going to allow them to maintain or even enhance their important role in the modern national governance systems, and contribute substantially to the management of the big, multi-dimensional and complex problems that modern societies face. In this direction this paper describes and evaluates a first attempt of the Greek Parliament to use two advanced ICTs, arguments visualization and structured e-forum (presented later in the third section), for increasing the quantity and quality of public participation in the legislation formation process. Both these technologies have a common theoretical foundation (the theoretical work on the 'wicked problems' and the use of 'Issue Based Information Systems' (IBIS) for supporting argumentative approaches for solving them, outlined in the following section) and aim to structure electronic information provision to citizens and consultation with them, respectively, and in this way improve them substantially. Taking into account that public participation in the legislation formation in order to be meaningful and effective necessitates citizens to be sufficiently informed on complex issues, usually analysed in lengthy parliamentary documents in a legal and technical language, the use of arguments visualization aims to provide this information to citizens in an easily understandable and structured schematic manner, promoting transparency and accountability. Furthermore, discussions (both traditional, in 'face-to-face' mode, or electronic) on legislation under formation between heterogeneous participants with different viewpoints, perspectives, concerns and interests, in order to be effective and productive, need to be focused, structured and based on the exchange of arguments and contra-arguments; the use of structured e-forum (instead of the usual simple unstructured e-forum) aims to structure the electronic consultations on legislation under formation among stakeholders (i.e. among all affecting or affected by this legislation) and make it more substantial and argumentative, promoting interaction with society, accessibility and representativeness. The research presented in this paper has been conducted as part of the LEX-IS project ('Enabling Participation of the Youth in the Public Debate of Legislation among Parliaments, Citizens and Businesses in the European Union') (www.lex-is.eu) supported by the 'eParticipation' Preparatory Action of the European Commission.[5]

---

[5] E. Loukis, M. Wimmer, Y. Charalabidis, A. Triantafillou and R. Gatautis, 'Argumentation systems and ontologies for enhancing public participation in the legislation process', *EGOV 2007 International Conference*, Regensburg, Germany, 3–7 September 2007.

This paper is organized in six sections. The following section outlines our theoretical background, followed by the third section describing the technological platform we developed with the above advanced features. In the fourth section is described the evaluation methodology, and in the fifth section the evaluation results. Finally, in the sixth section the conclusions are summarized and future research directions are suggested.

Theoretical Background

Rittel and Weber in their highly influential paper discussing 'Dilemmas in a General Theory of Planning'[6] point out that the nature of public policy problems tends to change dramatically. Previously, though they were not trivial, they were 'tame', with this term denoting that they had more clear and widely accepted definitions and objectives, so they could be solved by professionals using 'first generation' methods, which resemble the ones used in natural sciences and engineering, and are based on the idea of 'efficiency'; in particular these methods focus on achieving some predefined objectives with the lowest possible resources through mathematical optimization algorithms. This approach has been successful in solving well-defined problems associated with basic needs and problems of society, for example, with building basic infrastructures and services, such as electricity and water provision, education, etc. However, as societies tend to become more heterogeneous and pluralistic in terms of culture, values, concerns and lifestyles, their public policy problems tend to become 'wicked', this term denoting that they lack clear and widely agreed definitions and objectives, and are characterized by high complexity and many stakeholders with different and heterogeneous problem views, values and concerns. The above paper identifies 10 characteristics of these wicked problems, which differentiate them from the tame ones, and necessitate a different approach to solving them:

- There is no definitive formulation of a wicked problem.
- Wicked problems have no stopping rule (like the ones of the natural sciences and engineering), so planners stop for reasons which are external to the problem, for example, running out of time or money.
- Solutions to wicked problems are not 'true-or-false', but 'good-or-bad', and this judgement is not 'objective', but highly 'subjective', depending on the group or personal interests of the judges and their special value-sets.
- There is no immediate and ultimate test of a solution to a wicked problem (this requires examination of several types of impacts on numerous persons or groups, and for a long time period).
- Every solution to a wicked problem is a 'one-shot' operation; every attempt counts significantly and there is no opportunity to learn by trial-and-error.
- Wicked problems do not have an enumerable (or an exhaustively describable) set of potential solutions, nor is there a well-described set of permissible operations that may be incorporated into the plan.
- Every wicked problem is essentially unique (despite seeming similarities among wicked problems, one can never be certain that the particulars of a

---

[6] H. W. J. Rittel and M. M. Weber, 'Dilemmas in a general theory of planning', *Policy Sciences*, 4, 1973, pp. 155–169.

problem do not override its commonalities with other problems already dealt with).
- A wicked problem usually can be considered as a symptom of another 'higher level' problem, so defining the boundaries and the level at which such a problem will be addressed is of critical importance.
- The existence of a discrepancy between the real state of affairs and a desired/targeted one which constitutes a wicked problem can be explained in numerous ways, and the choice of explanation determines the nature of the problem's resolution.
- The public policy planner has no right to be wrong, as the consequences will be severe for many citizens.

For these reasons the wicked problems cannot be solved only by using mathematical algorithms that calculate 'optimal' solutions, since they lack basic pre-conditions for this: they do not have clear and widely agreed definitions (with each stakeholder usually having a different view of it) and objectives (which could be used as criteria for evaluating possible solutions). So they cannot be addressed through the above 'technocratic' first generation methods; for this reason Rittel and Weber in the above-mentioned influential paper suggest that wicked problems require a different 'second generation' approach, which combines public participation with technocratic analysis by experts. In particular, its first and fundamental phase is consultation and argumentation among problem stakeholders, during which discourse, reasoning and negotiation take place, aiming to synthesize different views and formulate a shared definition of the problem and the objectives to be achieved; having this as a base it is then possible in a second phase to proceed to a technocratic analysis by experts (e.g. using mathematical optimization algorithms for the defined problem).

Further research on this participative/argumentative approach to the solution of public policy problems resulted later in the development of the 'Issue Based Information Systems' (IBIS) concept[7] as a means to support with ICT its application; such a system aims to 'stimulate a more scrutinized style of reasoning which more explicitly reveals the arguments. It should help identify the proper questions, to develop the scope of positions in response to them, and assist in generating dispute.' IBIS are based on a simple but powerful discussion model, whose main elements are 'topics' (meant as broad discussion areas), 'questions' (particular issues–problems to be addressed within the discussion topic—they can be factual, deontic, explanatory or instrumental), 'ideas' (possible answers–solutions to questions) and 'arguments' (evidence or viewpoints that support or object to ideas).

However, there are only a few previous publications describing the use of structured electronic discussion tools based on the IBIS framework for public policy consultations,[8] while quite limited is the research that has been conducted

---

[7] W. Kunz and H. Rittel, 'Issues as elements of information systems', Working Paper No. 131, University of California, Berkeley, 1979; J. Conklin and M. Begeman, 'gIBIS: a tool for all reasons', *Journal of the American Society for Information Science*, 40(3), 1989, pp. 200–213; J. Conklin, 'Dialog mapping: reflections on an industrial strength case study', in P. Kirschner, S. Buckingham Shum and C. Carr (eds), *Visualizing Argumentation: Software Tools for Collaborative and Educational Sense-Making*, Springer-Verlag, London, 2003.

[8] N. Karacapilidis and D. Papadias, 'Computer supported argumentation and collaborative

concerning the systematic evaluation of such structured tools.[9] Also, some research has been conducted on the use of the IBIS framework for the visualization (schematic representation) of the main points of political dialogues, so that they can be easily understood by the public.[10] Therefore, further research is required concerning the application of this framework for structuring electronic information provision and consultation in real-life public policy problems, and its systematic evaluation.

It should be emphasized that the problems of legislation formation are highly wicked, since they are characterized by high complexity (in most laws under formation there are many interrelated issues to be regulated) and many stakeholder groups, with each of them having quite different views of the problem, values and interests, which are very often in conflict with one another. For these reasons legislation formation necessitates a high level of well-organized and wide participation of all stakeholders and efficient consultation among them. However, this is not possible due to time limitations, so most parliaments for each bill under discussion usually invite in the competent parliamentary committee only a few representatives of the most important stakeholders, give them some time to express their opinions and allow them only some limited interaction with MPs (usually they answer MPs' questions). Using appropriate ICT tools both the quantity and the quality of stakeholders' participation can be considerably increased, resulting in better, more balanced and applicable legislation.

Description of the Technical Platform

The Greek Parliament at the beginning of the LEX-IS project had already a website,[11] which provided extensive information about the legal framework of its operation and the Greek Constitution, the MPs (CVs and activities) and also all the documents of the legislation that has been passed or is under discussion (justification report, initial document, report of the first discussion in the competent parliamentary committee, amendments, final document). However, this website did not have a space for e-consultations on bills under discussion for

---

Footnote 8 continued
decision making: the HERMES system', *Information Systems*, 26(4), 2001, pp. 259–277; T. F. Gordon and N. Karacapilidis, 'The Zeno argumentation framework', paper presented at the Sixth International Conference on Artificial Intelligence and Law (ICAIL '97), 1997.

[9] N. Karacapilidis, E. Loukis and S. Dimopoulos, 'Computer-supported G2G collaboration for public policy and decision making', *Journal of Enterprise Information Management*, 18(5), 2005, pp. 602–624; A. Xenakis and E. Loukis, 'An investigation of the use of structured e-Forum for enhancing e-Participation in parliaments', *International Journal of Electronic Governance*, 3(2), 2010, pp. 134–147.

[10] A. Renton, 'Seeing the point of politics: exploring the use of CSAV techniques as aids to understanding the content of political debates in the Scottish Parliament', *Artificial Intelligence and Law*, 14, 2006, pp. 277–304; A. Renton and A. Macintosh, 'Computer supported argument maps as a policy memory', *Information Society Journal*, 23(2), 2007, pp. 125–133; R. Ohl, 'Computer supported argument visualisation: modelling in consultative democracy around wicked problems', in A. Okada, S. Buckingham Shum and T. Sherborne (eds), *Knowledge Cartography: Software Tools and Mapping Techniques*, Springer-Verlag, London, 2008; E. Loukis, A. Xenakis and N. Tserpeli, 'Using argument visualization to enhance e-Participation in the legislation formation process', *IFIP First International Conference on e-Participation—ePart 2009*, Linz, Austria, September 2009.

[11] < www.hellenicparliament.gr >.

promoting e-participation. So it was decided to develop, as part of the LEX-IS project, an advanced e-consultations platform for extending the public participation in the legislation formation beyond the few stakeholders' representatives invited in the competent parliamentary committee, so that more representatives, and also simple citizens as well, can participate.

The basic component of this platform is a structured e-forum based on the IBIS framework, which requires participants to annotate semantically each new posting as 'issue', 'alternative', 'pro-argument', 'contra-argument' or 'comment'. This is expected to guide the participants to think in a more structured way about the bill under discussion (i.e. to think which are the main issues, what are the main alternatives for addressing each of them, which are the main advantages and disadvantages of each alternative, etc.), make more mentally processed and focused contributions, and finally increase the quality, focus and effectiveness of the discussion. Additionally, this structured e-forum tool requires each posting to be associated with a previous one according to some predefined rules based on IBIS: for each issue participants are allowed to enter other issues, alternatives or comments, for each alternative they can enter pro-arguments, contra-arguments or comments, for each argument (pro or contra) other arguments (pro or contra) and for each comment other comments. This is expected to improve the interaction and communication among the participants, and therefore increase further the quality, focus and effectiveness of the discussion.

Using this structured e-forum tool a pilot electronic consultation was held on a highly controversial bill under formation regulating the 'Contracts of Voluntary Cohabitation', which formalized an existing social situation in Greece for a long time: many couples, especially among the younger age groups, are reluctant to proceed directly to marriage, and instead choose to live together under the same roof for some time, and during that time have children, share living expenses and buy property. These couples were not legally bonded, leaving the weaker partner unprotected in case that such an informal cohabitation ends. In order to cover this legal gap this bill regulates the formalization of the voluntary cohabitation of couples, and also the issues arising when such unions are dissolved. It consists of 13 main articles and their titles are shown in Appendix A. In this pilot e-consultation 79 citizens participated, aged between 18 and 35 years old, coming mainly from the university and the parliament environment. In Figure 1 we can see a part of the discussion tree that has been formed (translated in English). In total were entered 8 'issues', 15 'alternatives', 13 'comments', 35 'pro-arguments' and 60 'con-arguments'.

This platform includes also a space providing background information to the participants in the e-consultations about the bill under discussion. In particular, the participants of this pilot were provided with the following documents:

(a) the justification report of the bill, which is authored by the proposing competent Ministry and includes the main problems and reasons that necessitate the proposed law and the basic directions and solutions it provides;
(b) the content of the bill, which includes a number of articles, each of them settling a particular issue;
(c) the minutes of the discussion of this bill in the competent parliamentary committee, which includes the opinions and positions of the invited

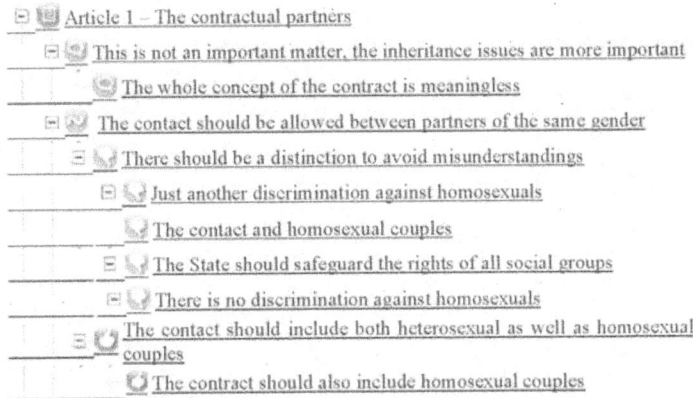

Figure 1. Part of the discussion tree formed in the structured e-forum.

stakeholders' representatives and experts, and also the ones of the parties' main speakers.

Additionally, in the same space were also provided visualizations of the main points of the above documents, which were based on the IBIS framework as well, constructed using the 'Compendium' tool.[12] Each of these visualizations had the form of a map of interconnected question nodes (issues, problems), idea nodes (solutions, settlements), argument nodes (positive ones corresponding to advantages and negative ones corresponding to disadvantages) and information nodes. These visualizations aimed to provide to the participants the information of the corresponding lengthy and difficult to understand documents in an easily understandable and structured schematic manner. In Figures 2–4 are shown the visualizations of the justification report, of one article of the bill and of the position of one political party, respectively.

Evaluation Methodology

Through a synthesis of elements from existing 'traditional' (offline) public participation evaluation frameworks[13] and e-participation evaluation frameworks,[14] and taking also into account the particular characteristics of the legislation formation process, a methodology for evaluating e-participation

---

[12] <compendium.open.ac.uk/institute>.

[13] C. Coglianese, 'Assessing consensus: the promise and performance of negotiated rulemaking', *Duke Law Journal*, 46(6), 1997, pp. 1255–1349; G. Rowe and L. J. Frewer, 'Public participation methods: a framework for evaluation', *Science, Technology, & Human Values*, 25(1), 2000, pp. 3–29; G. Rowe and L. J. Frewer, 'Evaluating public-participation exercises: a research agenda', *Science, Technology, & Human Values*, 29(4), 2004, pp. 512–557; G. Rowe, R. Marsch and L. J. Frewer, 'Evaluation of a deliberative conference using validated criteria', *Science, Technology, & Human Values*, 29(1), 2004, pp. 88–121; OECD (Organization for Economic Co-operation & Development), *Evaluating Public Participation in Policy Making*, OECD Publication Service, Paris, 2004.

[14] A. Whyte and A. Macintosh, 'Analysis and evaluation of e-consultations', *e-Service Journal*, 2(1), 2003, pp. 9–34; OECD, *Promise and Problems of e-Democracy: Challenges of Online Citizen Engagement*, OECD Publication Service, Paris, 2003; A. Macintosh and A. Whyte, 'Evaluating how e-participation changes local participation', *eGovernment Workshop '06 (eGOV06)*, Brunel University, London,

Figure 2. Visualization of the justification report.

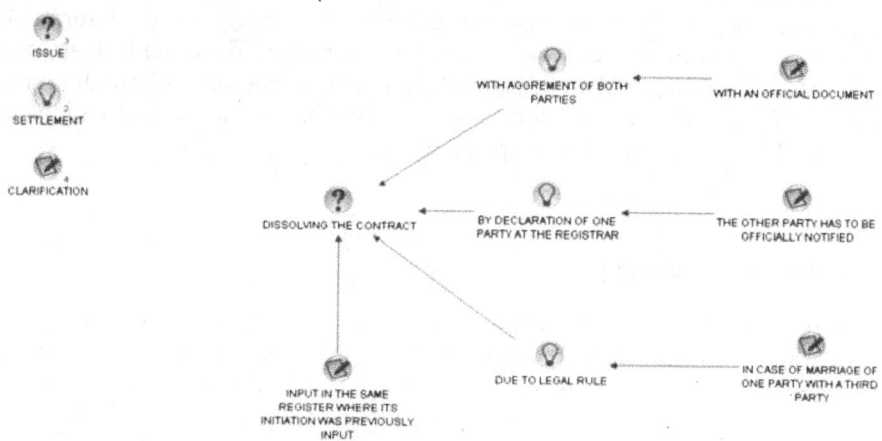

Figure 3. Visualization of the fourth article of the bill (concerning the dissolution of a contract).

in parliaments was developed;[15] then an adaptation of it to the LEX-IS project was made, which is organized around four evaluation perspectives:

Footnote 14 continued
11 September 2006; A. Macintosh and A. Whyte, 'Towards an evaluation framework for eParticipation', *Transforming Government: People, Process & Policy*, 2(1), 2008, pp. 16–30.

[15] E. Loukis, A. Xenakis and Y. Charalabidis, 'An evaluation framework for e-Participation in parliaments', *International Journal of Electronic Governance*, 3(1), 2010, pp. 25–45; E. Loukis and A. Xenakis, 'A framework for evaluating e-Participation in the legislation development process', *EGOV 2008 International Conference*, Torino, Italy, 31 August–5 September 2008.

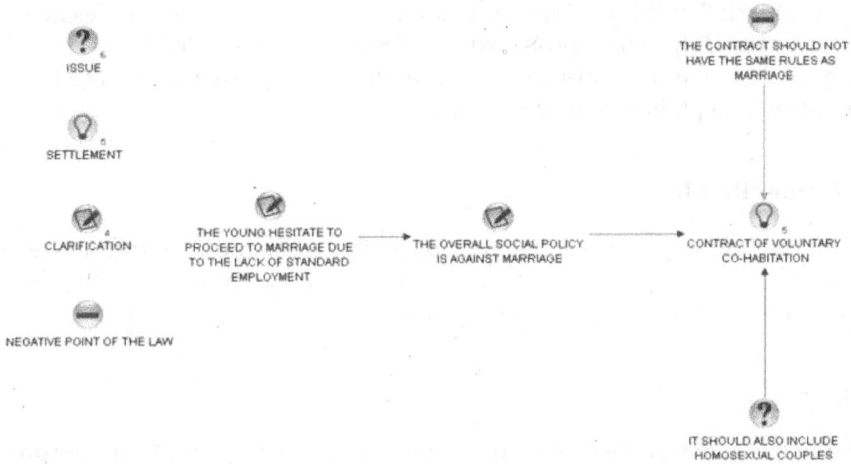

Figure 4. Visualization of the position of one political party.

i) Context (CONT) (aiming to assess important characteristics of the context in which the pilot has taken place)
ii) Process (PRO) (aiming to assess the process that has been followed in the pilot)
iii) System (SYS) (aiming to assess the technical platform)
iv) Outcomes (OUT) (aiming to assess the outcomes of this pilot from a political viewpoint).

These four perspectives were used as a basis for both quantitative (using a questionnaire) and qualitative (by a focus group of participants, officials of the Greek Parliament and MPs' assistants) evaluation. As part of the former for each perspective a number of evaluation criteria have been defined, which have been used for preparing a questionnaire for quantitative evaluation, shown in Appendix B. The 'Context' perspective includes a number of questions assessing the demographic characteristics of participants (age, gender and education) and their extent of interest in the bill under discussion. The 'Process' perspective includes a number of questions assessing the extent of having informed the participants about the purpose and objectives of this project, the participants and their role; the extent of having sufficient and appropriate rules and management in this e-consultation, and adequacy of time for getting informed on the bill and then for discussing electronically about it; and the quality of information provided to the participants about the bill, with the main emphasis on the visualizations. The 'System' perspective includes a number of questions assessing how easy it was to learn and use the platform, with the emphasis on the structured e-forum tool, and the appropriateness of the tools and technologies deployed in the platform for supporting e-participation. Finally, the 'Outcomes' perspective includes a number of questions assessing the extent of platform usage (frequency of platform usage and contributions, usage of the visualizations, etc.), the perceived quality of contributions and learning from them, the perceived impact achieved on the particular legislation, the participants' satisfaction and their intention to participate again in similar e-consultations in the future.

We remark that this evaluation methodology covers both the 'efficiency' and 'effectiveness' dimensions proposed by relevant ICT evaluation literature;[16] also it covers both the 'ease-of-use' and 'usefulness' dimensions proposed by the technology acceptance models literature.[17]

Evaluation Results

In this section we present the results of the evaluation of the above four perspectives of this pilot e-consultation, based on a synthesis of the evidence collected from both the quantitative and the qualitative parts of it.

Context

Initially we analysed the context of the pilot, which is important for interpreting the findings from the evaluation of the other three perspectives of it: this has shown that the participants were young (80 per cent of them were 21–30 years old, while the remaining 20 per cent were 31–40 years old) and highly educated (60 per cent were university graduates, while the remaining 40 per cent had postgraduate education as well), with a small overrepresentation of males (60 per cent) in comparison with females; also, a very large majority of the participants found the topic under discussion interesting and very important or important.

Process

As a next step we analysed the process of this pilot e-consultation. In general it can be concluded that there was a good organization of the pilot, resulting in a good understanding by a large majority of the participants about the objectives, the participants and their role. Most of the participants found that there was appropriate management rules in the electronic discussion and sufficient time, and also that sufficient and objective information was provided to them about the bill under discussion. With respect to clarity, most participants found that the information provided to them was clear to a very good (16 per cent) or good extent (44 per cent), but a considerable extent perceive a medium (36 per cent) or even small (4 per cent) level of clarity of these parliamentary documents (Figure 5). Taking into account the above-mentioned high educational level of the participants, this result shows the inherent difficulty that non-experts have in understanding such parliamentary documents usually written in a complex, legal and technical language (we expect that for an 'average' citizen there will be more difficulties).

This makes the visualization of the main points of these documents necessary if we want to achieve a wider dissemination and discussion of them. The majority

---

[16] S. Smithson and R. Hirschheim, 'Analysing information systems evaluation: another look at an old problem', *European Journal of Information Systems*, 7, 1998, pp. 158–174.

[17] F. D. Davis, 'Perceived usefulness, perceived ease of use, and user acceptance of information technology', *MIS Quarterly*, 13(3), 1989, pp. 319–339; V. Venkatesh and F. D. Davis, 'A theoretical extension of the technology acceptance model: four longitudinal field studies', *Management Science*, 45(2), 2000, pp. 186–204; V. Venkatesh, M. G. Morris, G. B. Davis and F. D. Davis, 'User acceptance of information technology: toward a unified view', *MIS Quarterly*, 27(3), 2003, pp. 425–478.

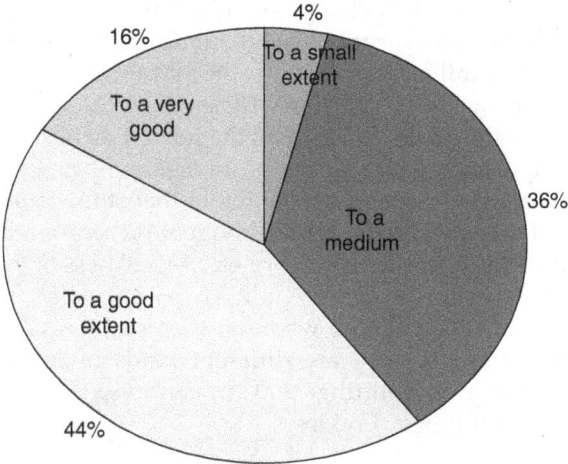

Figure 5. Perceived clarity of the information provided to the participant on the bill.

of the participants found these visualizations very easy (32 per cent) or easy (24 per cent) or rather easy (40 per cent) to understand, while nobody found them rather difficult and only a few (4 per cent) found them difficult to understand (Figure 6).

Similar are the conclusions from the more specific questions on this, which reveal that the visualizations were very helpful for understanding the justification report and the content (articles) of the bill, and also the positions/opinions of the experts invited and five political parties present in the Greek Parliament. Also, a large majority of the participants (96 per cent) found the visualizations sufficient for understanding the main points of this bill and did not have to open the corresponding textual documents.

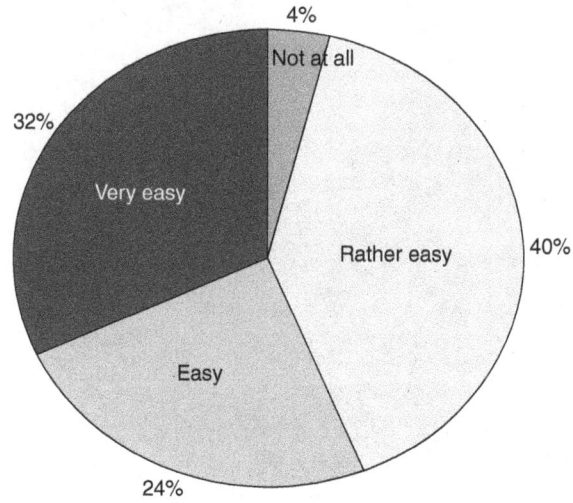

Figure 6. Perceived ease of understanding the visualizations.

All the persons who participated in the qualitative discussion in the focus group agreed that the visualizations were understandable to them, after a learning period of familiarization with the symbols. The advantages of visualizations were proved to be the time efficiencies created for the participants who did not have the time to go through all the related texts provided. They also mentioned that the visualizations of the positions/opinions of the experts and the political parties were more understandable than the visualizations of the content (articles) of the law and its justification report (because the latter are in a more legal/technical language than the former). A weakness of the visualizations of the articles of the law came from the opinion of a legal expert, who argued that all the types of settlements included were represented by a single type of node ('settlement node'), though there are different kinds of legal rules, such as prohibitive, imperative, permitting and presumptions, which should be represented by different types of nodes.

System

Next we focused on the system (technical platform) that was used in this pilot e-consultation. In general, a large majority of the participants found it easy (84 per cent) or very easy (4 per cent), while quite a low percentage of the participants had a negative perception on this (12 per cent) (Figure 7).

However, if we focus on the most innovative component of it, the structured e-forum, a different picture is revealed. Only a small percentage of the participants (12 per cent) found it easy to use the structured e-forum (i.e. to correctly characterize an idea as an issue, an alternative, a pro-argument, a contra-argument or a comment, and then correctly associate it with a previous

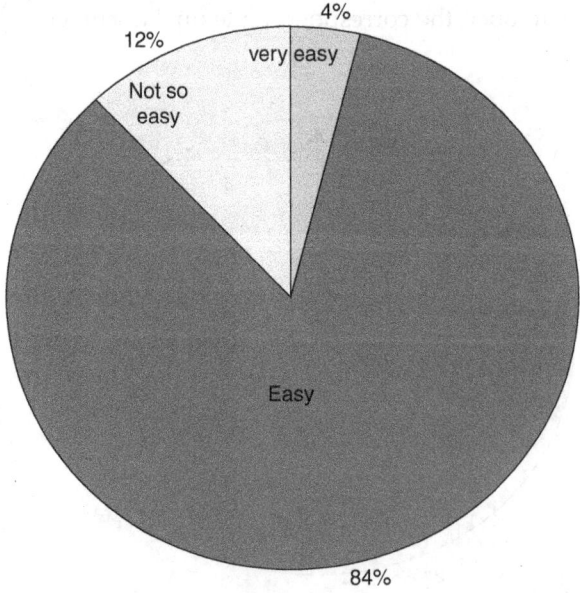

Figure 7. Perceived ease of use of the system.

posting according to the rules), while most found it 'medium to easy' (68 per cent) and a considerable percentage 'medium to difficult' (20 per cent) (Figure 8). Taking into account the high educational level of the participants, this result shows the inherent difficulty of using such a structured discussion tool (we expect that an 'average' education citizen will have more difficulties). This is due to the considerable mental effort required in order to think in the structured way that such a tool imposes, that is, to think which are the main issues, what are the main alternatives for addressing each of them, which are the main advantages and disadvantages of each alternative, etc., before entering a posting.

More clear is the picture with respect to the 'usefulness' of the structured e-forum, as a large majority of the participants (92 per cent) found it much better or a little better than the usual unstructured e-forum (in which there is no characterization/annotation of postings). This indicates that such a structured discussion tool results in more mentally processed, thoughtful, focused and therefore higher quality contributions by the participants; this is also due to the fact that these contributions are better associated with the ones of the other participants, so a better interaction among them is achieved, in comparison with the unstructured discussions taking place in the usual unstructured e-forum tools. Furthermore, a large majority of the participants found that the tools and technologies deployed in this technical platform are appropriate for promoting e-participation (both for informing citizens and for engaging them in productive online discussions), offering benefits not found in the 'traditional' participation and attracting citizens to use the platform again.

The persons who participated in the focus group qualitative discussion agreed that overall the use of the structured e-forum was a strength of the pilot, since it enables a more focused, productive and effective e-discussion. However, at the same time they emphasized some important difficulties for its users: (a) the difficulty of the correct assignment of type to the content of postings

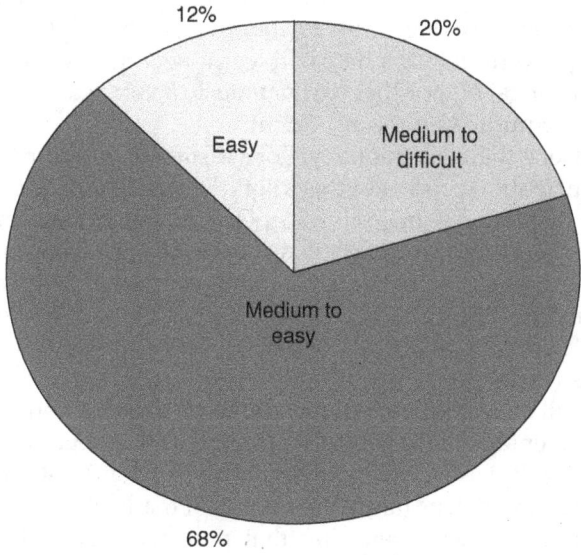

Figure 8. Perceived ease of use of the structured e-forum.

(an examination of the participants' postings in this e-consultation revealed that about 10 per cent of them had mistaken assignment of type, which confirms this difficulty), (b) the difficulty of wording appropriately the title of each posting, which is directly shown in the discussion tree of the structured e-forum box (while the full description of the posting is shown in another box only if its title is clicked in the tree), so that it reflects the content of the posting. Another problem mentioned was associated with the moderation of the postings: from the time one posting was entered by a user it usually took five to six hours until the moderator approved it and the posting became visible; so it was not possible for this user to see it immediately, and possibly enter more postings associated with it, while other users could see it only after a long delay. Additionally, some weaknesses of the user interface were mentioned, for example, the platform should provide more space (i.e. a bigger box) for the structured e-forum, so that the users do not have to use so much scrolling up and down when trying to access previous participants' postings; also, the above-mentioned documentation and visualizations of the bill needed to be downloaded first over the Internet from the LEX-IS platform to the user's computer, then opened and studied separately, and afterwards the user had to enter the forum to make a posting, causing a lot inconvenience, so it was suggested that this informative material should be directly accessible by the user on a single 'click' in separate HTML pages.

Outcome

Finally we analysed the outcome of this pilot e-consultation. The extent of use of the platform by the participants (visits, use of informative material, postings) was satisfactory. A large majority of the participants characterize the quality of the contributions (postings) in this e-consultation as medium to high (76 per cent), a smaller percentage (16 per cent) as high and an even smaller percentage as medium to low (8 per cent) (Figure 9). Furthermore, a very high percentage of the participants (96 per cent) felt that they had learnt new things and ideas from the contributions (postings) of the other participants to a very good (4 per cent), good (44 per cent) or medium (40 per cent) extent.

For these reasons there is a high level of satisfaction of the participants with the whole e-participation process in this pilot (Figure 10) and also with their role in this process, and a large majority (96 per cent) would continue using this platform being interested to participate in such an e-consultation again. However, the participants felt uncertain about the impact of their contributions in this e-consultation on the legislation under discussion (i.e. on the final form of the law on the 'Contracts of Voluntary Cohabitation'); most of the participants (72 per cent) responded that they did not know whether the ideas and visions they expressed will be further considered and have an impact on this law, while a much smaller percentage had a positive feeling on this (20 per cent) (Figure 11). This feeling is probably associated (at least to some extent) with the low level of trust that many Greek citizens (and also citizens of many other countries as well) have in the political system, believing that politicians do not listen to them sufficiently, but are influenced mainly by a few economically and/or politically strong pressure groups.

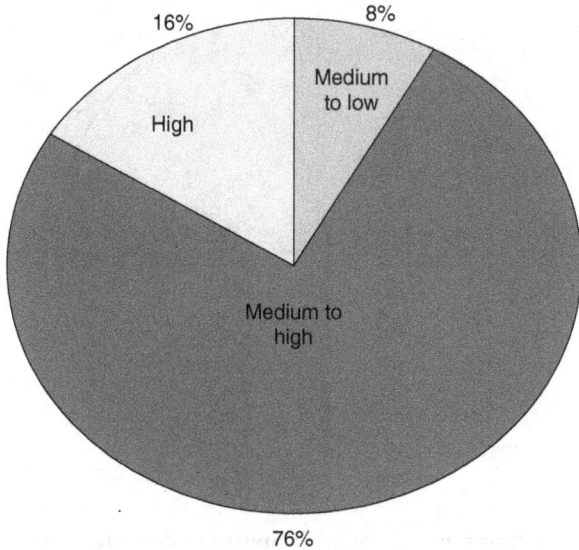

Figure 9. Perceived quality of contributions (postings).

In the focus groups' qualitative discussion there was a wide agreement that such e-consultations can be in the future a very useful and cost-effective tool for collecting opinions about bills under discussion from a wider group of people than the few (due to time limitations) representatives of the most important stakeholders invited in the parliamentary committees. The parliamentary officials and the MPs' assistants concluded that such tools can be useful to get the feel of public opinion on the issues discussed. Also, it has been stressed that such structured e-consultation tools can facilitate higher quality and more focused discussions.

However, it was pointed out that the political tradition in Greece is the Parliament for formulating the laws to take seriously into account the opinions

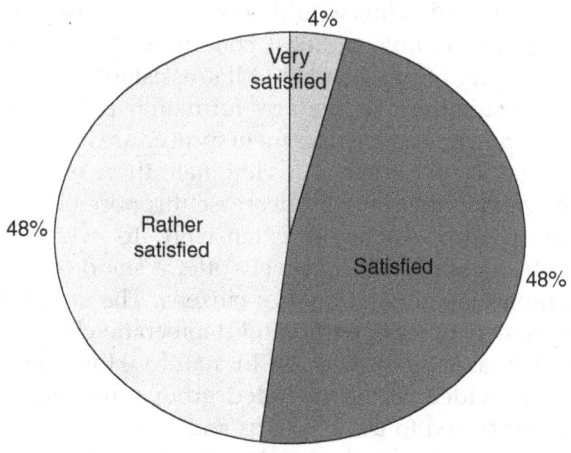

Figure 10. Level of satisfaction of the participants.

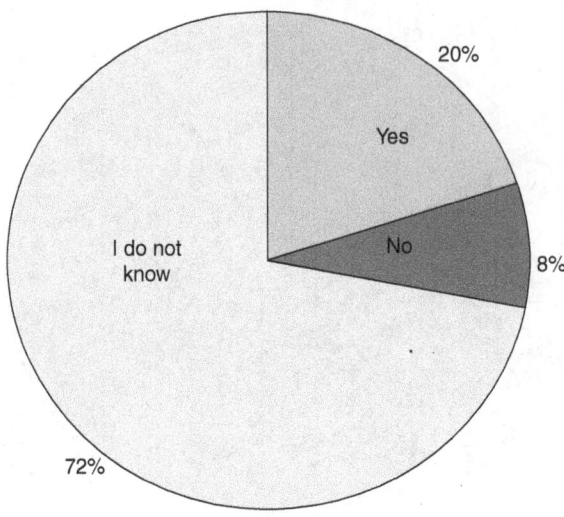

Figure 11. Beliefs of participants concerning the impact of their ideas and visions on the law.

of representatives of large stakeholder groups (e.g. presidents of chambers, associations, trade unions, etc.), who are not anonymous (so they are more responsible in expressing opinions), have a good experience and knowledge on the law under discussion and represent large numbers of affected citizens. On the contrary the opinions of 'simple' individuals, for whom we do not know how representative their opinions are, and to what extent they have experience and knowledge on the law under discussion, are taken into account to a much lower extent. Some of the participating students in this discussion argued that sometimes 'simple' individuals, who are anonymous and do not have any titles and responsibilities, can give to the parliament valuable information about thoughts, opinions and ideas in the society (or particular groups of it) concerning a law under discussion. However, this poses the risk of small extreme or even malicious groups attempting to use such e-participation platforms in order to impose their opinions and positions on the law discussed and promote their private agendas; all agreed that this would decrease the parliamentary usefulness and potential of such electronic political communication channels. For these reasons the parliamentary officials and the MPs' assistants would be reluctant to introduce such e-consultations in the law formation process unless properly protected through appropriate management procedures against extreme and malicious groups that would attempt to dominate these e-discussions; a wide participation of citizens in them would decrease this possibility.

The focus group also discussed extensively to what extent such an e-participation platform could prospectively offer a stand to the less powerful, excluded and non-participating in politics citizens. The structured forum was accepted as a discussion process with valid democratic characteristics and the Internet as a publicly accessible medium by nature. However, the technology would have to be provided to the excluded groups, invitations to contribute would have to be addressed to these groups and anonymity of opinions would have to be overcome in order for the postings to be seriously considered. Also, non-participating citizens who have a mistrust of the political system would still have to be persuaded that the new means are equally followed by a new attitude of the law formulation process owners towards public opinion on the contents of a law under formation. Furthermore, the inherent difficulty of participating in such structured e-consultations (need for extensive processing of thoughts) might reduce the participation of individuals of lower education, so that higher education groups will finally dominate and promote their positions and agendas.

Finally, it was concluded that a good solution would be for the Parliament for each law under discussion to organize two e-consultations: (i) a closed one in a structured e-forum for particular invited eponym representatives of large stakeholder groups, such as presidents of chambers, associations, trade unions, etc., and experts, enabling a larger number of them to participate and a more focused and in-depth discussion to take place, and (ii) an open one in a usual unstructured e-forum tool for anonymous individuals, who want to express their personal opinion.

Conclusions

In the previous sections of this paper has been described and evaluated the first attempt of the Greek Parliament to increase the quantity and quality of public participation in the legislation formation process using two advanced ICTs, computer supported arguments visualization and structured e-forum, which are based on previous theoretical work on the wicked problems and the argumentative approach to solving them. Initially the technical platform developed for this purpose has been presented. Its basic component is a structured e-forum tool, in which structured e-consultations can take place; it requires from the participants according to the IBIS theoretical framework: (i) to annotate semantically each new posting as issue, alternative, pro-argument, contra-argument or comment, and (ii) to associate it to a previous posting according to predefined rules: for each issue it is allowed to enter other issues, alternatives or comments, for each alternative to enter pro-arguments, contra-argument or comments, for each argument (pro or contra) other arguments (pro or contra) and for each comment other comments. This imposes a higher structure and organization in the e-consultation. Another important component of this technical platform is an information space providing background information to the participants in the e-consultations about the bill under discussion: this includes both the main documents of it (justification report, main content (articles), report of the discussion in the competent parliamentary committee) in textual form and also visualizations of their main points based on the IBIS theoretical framework. These visualizations had the form of maps of interconnected question nodes (issues, problems), idea nodes (solutions, settlements), argument nodes (positive ones corresponding to advantages and negative ones corresponding to disadvantages) and information nodes; they aim to present the most important information of the corresponding documents in an easily understandable and structured schematic manner. Using this technical platform a pilot e-consultation was held on a highly controversial bill concerning the 'Contracts of Voluntary Cohabitation'. For evaluating it a multi-perspective evaluation methodology was developed, through a synthesis of elements from existing traditional public participation and e-participation evaluation frameworks, taking also into account the particular characteristics of the legislation formation process. It includes four evaluation perspectives, the context, the process, the system and the outcomes of the e-consultation, which have been used both for quantitative and qualitative evaluation of the pilot.

It has been concluded that the visualizations of the main parliamentary documents (justification reports, main content/articles, minutes of discussions in parliamentary committees) are understandable and also can convey the main points of the above documents to a good extent; the only exception identified was in the visualizations of the bill articles, in which the settlement type of nodes seems too generic and has to be broken into several subtypes representing the various kind of legal rules included in a bill, such as prohibitive, imperative, permitting and presumptions. Therefore, the use of computer supported arguments visualization technologies seems to have a good potential in this area: they allow more citizens to be informed about the main points of legislation under formation and the opinions/positions of the political parties and knowledgeable experts on it, without having to spend too much time on this, or to be familiar with the complex legal and technical language of the parliamentary documents. In modern societies the main problems/issues which are regulated by parliaments tend to be highly complex and multi-dimensional, and 'simple citizens' find it difficult to understand them, so they tend to withdraw from the public discussion on them, leaving them to the representatives, the experts and the organized pressure groups. This can undermine public participation in the formation of legislation and finally result in 'unbalanced' legislation, which takes into account and incorporates mainly the agendas and interests of some social groups (e.g. organized minorities) and minimally the ones of some others. The use of computer supported arguments visualization technologies has the potential to counter this trend, reducing the effort and time requirements of being informed on current political debates, promoting two fundamental values of parliaments: transparency and accountability.

At the same time these visualizations include and focus the attention of the citizens on the 'substance' of the parliamentary documents: the main problems/issues they identify, the solutions they propose together with their advantages and disadvantages, and 'filter out' the excessive political rhetoric or other irrelevant material. Taking into account that the political debate in Greece (and in many other countries as well) has been criticized for having too much political rhetoric, generalities and lack of specific positions, solutions and arguments on the problems and needs of the society, these technologies have the potential to contribute to the improvement of the quality of both online and offline political debate, making it more substantial and argumentative. However, in order to have these important benefits it is necessary that these visualizations are constructed by a highly skilled, neutral and trusted group, so that they include the really important points but are not overloaded with too much detail, and at the same time they do not hide something important. For Greece we believe that the Legal Service of the Parliament (which processes all bills coming to the Parliament in order to identify legal problems or problems of incompliance to the Constitution), possibly in cooperation with a university, would be the most appropriate entities for constructing these visualizations.

Another interesting conclusion is that the use of a structured e-forum tool can considerably improve the quality of e-consultations in comparison with the usual unstructured e-forum tool. This is because the former guides the participants to think in a more structured way about the bill (or in general the topic) under discussion than the latter: it guides them initially to identify which are the main problems/issues, then to search for possible solutions to them, and finally to examine the main advantages and disadvantages of them. Additionally the structured e-forum tool guides the participants to associate each new posting with a previous one according to predefined rules, and in this way it improves the interaction among the participants. Therefore, the structured e-forum drives the participants to make more mentally processed and focused contributions, increasing the quality, focus and effectiveness of the discussion. This conclusion is in agreement with the ones of previous studies of other mechanisms of structuring electronic discussion and cooperation, such as moderation, scripts providing guidance to participants, different leadership styles,[18] which conclude that these structuring mechanisms have a positive impact on the efficiency and effectiveness of discussion and cooperation. For the above reasons the use of a structured e-forum by parliaments has the potential not only to widen public participation on legislation under formation (beyond the few stakeholders' representatives invited in the competent parliamentary committee) but also to improve its quality (leading to e-consultations with more substance, arguments and coherence), promoting two fundamental values of parliaments: accessibility and representativeness.

However, the adoption of such e-consultation tools by parliaments might increase the existing and widely debated 'digital divide'.[19] Some groups of modern societies (e.g. people of low income, low education or old age) do not have access to ICTs and competences to use them, and this limits their capabilities to participate in the highly ICT-dependent modern economy and society, and finally increases the already existing social inequalities and 'divides'. Therefore, these groups will not be able to benefit from such electronic information provision and consultation tools provided by the parliaments and from the participation opportunities they create, and this will increase further their handicaps and disadvantages with respect other groups having ICT access and competences. Also, taking into account that as concluded from our evaluation the structured e-forum is not easy to use, due to the considerable mental effort required in order to think in the structured way it imposes, it might be less suitable for and usable by lower education groups of the society. Therefore, the above-mentioned benefits it provides (increase of the quantity and quality of public participation in the legislation formation) might be limited to the higher education groups, and this will be another factor increasing the

---

[18] G. Mark, J. Grudin and S. Poltrock, 'Meeting at the desktop: an empirical study of virtually collocated teams', in *Proceedings of the Sixth European Conference on Computer-Supported Cooperative Work*, Kluwer Academic, Norwell, MA, 1999; S. Farnham, H. R. Chesley, D. E. McGhee and R. Kawal, 'Structured online interactions: improving the decision-making of small discussion groups', in *Proceedings of ACM 2000 Conference on Computer-Supported Cooperative Work (CSCW 2000)*, ACM Press, New York, 2000; S. Kahai, J. Fjermestad, S. Zhang and B. J. Avolio, 'Leadership in virtual teams: past, present, and future', *International Journal of E-Collaboration*, 3(1), 2007, pp. 1–8.

[19] OECD, *Learning to Bridge the Digital Divide*, OECD Publication Service, Paris, 2000; P. Norris, *Digital Divide: Civic Engagement, Information Poverty, and the Internet Worldwide*, Cambridge University Press, New York, 2001; K. Mossberger, C. J. Tolbert and M. Stansbury, *Virtual Inequality: Beyond the Digital Divide*, Georgetown University Press, Washington, DC, 2003; OECD, *The e-Government Imperative*, OECD Publication Service, Paris, 2003.

existing digital divide. Another problem of such e-consultations is that the participants are anonymous, so we do not know how representative are the positions/opinions expressed by each of them, and how much experience and knowledge on the topic under discussion each of them has; also, it is possible these e-consultations are finally dominated by small extreme or even malicious organized groups who want to impose their positions and agendas.

For reducing the above risks parliaments can organize for each bill under discussion several e-consultations with various levels of structure and for different target groups. In particular a closed e-consultation can be organized in a structured IBIS-based e-forum for particular invited eponym representatives of large stakeholder groups, such as presidents of chambers, associations, trade unions, experts and MPs of the competent parliamentary committee. Additionally, an open e-consultation can be organized in a usual unstructured e-forum tool for anonymous individuals, who want to express their personal opinion. Furthermore, some thematic (i.e. focusing on particular important topics) open e-consultations can be organized in e-forum tools of lower structure; they can be based either on the IBIS model, or on other less structured ones, such as the 'question–answer–comment' model,[20] which is easier for the participants and demands less metal effort from them. At the same time a good promotion of these e-consultations can ensure a wide participation of citizens, so that it is difficult for organized groups/minorities to dominate. Finally governments should continue, despite the economic crisis, their efforts to provide free ICT/Internet access and training to citizens who cannot afford it (e.g. in municipal Internet centres).

Euripidis Loukis is Assistant Professor of Information and Decision Support Systems at the University of the Aegean, Greece. Also, he is teaching e-Government at the National Academy of Public Administration. Formerly he has been Information Systems Advisor at the Ministry to the Presidency of Government, Technical Director of the 'Program for the Modernization of Greek Public Administration' of the Second European Union Support Framework and Representative of Greece at the Management Committees of the Programs IDA ('Interchange of Data between Administrations') and 'Telematics for Administration' of the European Union. He has participated in many international research programmes in the areas of e-government and e-participation, and has authored numerous journal and conference papers.

---

[20] E. Loukis and M. Wimmer, 'Analyzing different models of structured electronic consultation on legislation under formation', in *Proceedings of the 4th International Conference on Online Deliberation—OD 2010*, Leeds University Business School, Leeds, 30 June–2 July 2010.

Appendix A

Titles of the 13 main articles of the bill on 'Contracts of Voluntary Cohabitation':

(1) Establishment
(2) Pre-conditions
(3) Invalidity
(4) Dissolution
(5) Surname
(6) Possessions
(7) Palimony
(8) Fatherhood Presumption
(9) Children Surname
(10) Parental Care
(11) Inheritance Rights
(12) Suspension of Cancellation
(13) Application Scope.

Appendix B

Questionnaire of the quantitative evaluation:

I. Context

Q-CONT1: What is your age group?
Q-CONT2: What is your gender?
Q-CONT3: What is your educational level?
Q-CONT4: Do you find the topics discussed in the platform appealing and interesting?
Q-CONT5: How would you judge the importance of the topics discussed?

II. Process

Q-PRO1: Are you aware of the purpose and objectives of the LEX-IS project?
Q-PRO2: Was it clear who were the participants in this e-participation project and what was their role?
Q-PRO3: Were there sufficient and appropriate rules and management in this e-consultation?
Q-PRO4: Was there adequate time for getting informed on the law and then for discussing electronically about it on the platform?
Q-PRO5: Was the information provided to you about the law sufficient?
Q-PRO6: Was the information provided to you about the law understandable and clear?
Q-PRO7: Was the information provided to you about the law precise and objective?
Q-PRO8: Was it easy for you to understand the visualizations?
Q-PRO9: Were the visualizations enough or did you feel the need to access the reference text in order to understand them?

Q-PRO10: To what extent did the visualization of the justification report of the law help you to understand its content in a short timeframe?
Q-PRO11: To what extent did the visualization of the articles of the law help you to understand their content in a short timeframe?
Q-PRO12: To what extent did the visualization of the expert and party reports on the law help you to understand their content in a short timeframe?

III. System

Q-SYS1: Do you think the platform (the sum of tools and information provided online) is easy to use?
Q-SYS2: Do you think learning to operate the platform is unproblematic? Does the platform allow an intuitive handling?
Q-SYS3: How easy it was to use the structured forum (i.e. to correctly characterize your idea as an issue, an alternative, a pro-argument, a contra-argument or a comment, and then correctly enter it in the structured forum)?
Q-SYS4: How easy it was to access, read and understand the postings of the other participants (issues, alternatives, pro-arguments, contra-arguments, comments) and the connections among them in the structured forum?
Q-SYS5: What is your general assessment of the structured forum as a tool for important e-consultations in comparison to the normal forum tools (where you do not have to characterize your posting as an issue, an alternative, a pro-argument, a contra-argument or a comment, and then enter it correctly)?
Q-SYS6: Overall, would you say that the tools and technologies deployed in the platform are appropriate for the online participation in the project?
Q-SYS7: Overall, would you deem the tools and technologies deployed in the platform appropriate for the topic discussed?
Q-SYS8: Do you miss certain participation functionalities and services, which were not provided in the online platform but which you may know from other participation experiences?
Q-SYS9: Does the platform offer benefits you have not found in traditional participation, which attract you to use the platform again for having your say in democratic participation?
Q-SYS10: Does the platform provide proper participation tools to sufficiently inform you about the topics under discussion?
Q-SYS11: Does the platform provide proper participation tools and structuring mechanisms to engage in the online discussion of the topics?

IV. Outcome

Q-OUT1: How often did you visit the platform?
Q-OUT2: How often did you contribute, e.g. by posting an opinion, by participating in an opinion poll, etc.?
Q-OUT3: Will you come back to participate again after the project terminates?
Q-OUT4: Will you continue to use the platform?
Q-OUT5: How do you assess the quality of the contributions (postings) entered by the participants in this e-consultation?

Q-OUT6: To what extent did you learn new things and ideas from the contributions (postings) entered by the other participants in this e-consultation?
Q-OUT7: Through your contributions, did you reach an impact in the legislation theme discussed online?
Q-OUT8: Are you satisfied with the influence you achieved?
Q-OUT9: Do you think your ideas and visions will be further considered?
Q-OUT10: Does the result you have expected match the result you have received?
Q-OUT11: Do you like the role you are playing in the process?
Q-OUT12: How satisfied were you with the process?
Q-OUT13: Did you use the visualizations of the articles of the law, the expert reports and the party positions, provided in the platform?

Electronic participation pilots in the Western Balkans: lessons from the field

SOTIRIOS KOUSSOURIS, YANNIS CHARALABIDIS, LOUKAS KIPENIS, DIMITRIOS ASKOUNIS and ODETTA STAVRI

Introduction

Nowadays, the democracy deficit occurrence is strong as ostensibly democratic organizations or institutions in fact fall short of fulfilling what are believed to be the principles of democracy.[1] The political communication, instead of being a dialogue deliberation, tends to be monological, professionally produced and released for public consumption mainly based to a large extent on marketing criteria, so it needs a drastic revitalization, using all available means including advanced information and communication technologies (ICT).[2]

In this direction eParticipation can be defined as technology-mediated interaction between the citizens, the civil society, the administration and the formal political spheres, usually over some decision-making, legislation or simple deliberation process.[3] It is a field constantly changing and trying to mature in order to establish its own structures within the IT and decision-making community,[4] whereas its two main driving forces, technology and democracy, are also still in transition, a fact which is more obvious in converging countries like the ones of the Western Balkans. Those driving forces incorporate the necessary preconditions for a successful deployment of an e-participation system. Specifically, the technology acceptance of an e-participation system, in terms of full awareness, usefulness and ease of use for the users, constitutes a crucial factor for successful fulfilment of the goals of electronic participation. Furthermore, the impact of the system on the political process and the promotion of citizens' participation in government decision-making and political deliberation is the other crucial success factor.

This paper presents and evaluates a set of e-participation pilots conducted as part of Western Balkans Democracy Participation (WEB.DEP), a specific support

---

[1] L. Sanford, 'How the United States Constitution contributes to the democratic deficit in America', *Drake Law Review*, 55, 2007, pp. 859–885.

[2] E. Loukis, M. Wimmer, A. Triantafyllou, Y. Charalabidis, G. Gionis and R. Gatautis, 'A development of legislation through electronic support of participation: LEXIS', *eChallenges 2007 Conference*, 2007; E. Loukis, M. Wimmer, Y. Charalabidis, A. Triantafillou and R. Gatautis, 'Argumentation systems and ontologies for enhancing public participation in the legislation process', *EGOV 2007 International Conference*, Regensburg, Germany, 3–7 September 2007.

[3] C. Sanford and J. Rose, 'Characterizing eParticipation', *International Journal of Information Management*, 27, 2007, pp. 406–421.

[4] J. Rose and C. S. Sanford, 'Mapping eParticipation: four central research challenges', *Communications of the AIS*, 20(55), 2007, pp. 909–943.

action project,[5] funded under the European Commission's Sixth Framework Programme[6] with a view to using the Internet for strengthening democratic processes by increasing citizen involvement and media independence, and also for supporting cooperation between the Western Balkan countries. The project has been implemented by a consortium of seven organizations, including the national news-media agencies from Albania, Serbia and the Former Yugoslav Republic of Macedonia (FYROM), as well as organizations from two member states (Greece and the UK). The associated online initiative consisted of three national thematic portals in the above three countries, which contained community forums, integrated with the news systems and designed to support e-participation.

For evaluating these e-participation pilots we designed a methodology that focuses on the two factors, technology acceptance by the users (a traditional perspective of information systems research) and impact on citizens' participation (a traditional perspective of political sciences research). Each factor is evaluated by suitably designed questionnaires, and the responses are processed using statistical methods in order to draw conclusions from them.

This paper initially presents an overview of the evaluated system in the next section, while in the third section it presents the theoretical foundation of the evaluation methodology that has been followed. The fourth section elaborates on the evaluation of the results and finally the fifth section outlines conclusions and proposes future research directions.

The Western Balkans National News Agencies' eParticipation System

System Overview

The system we used for conducting these e-participation pilots consisted of three national thematic portals that enable sharing of news and public information. These portals also contained community forums, integrated with the news system and designed to support e-participation. The portals are hosted and managed by the following news agencies: Albanian Telegraphic Agency (ATA),[7] Macedonian Information Agency (MIA)[8] and National News Agency of the Republic of Serbia (TANJUG).[9] There is also a central forum,[10] in English, to facilitate regional interaction. The forums of the system are shown in Figure 1.

News agency journalists are able to start discussions in the English-language central forum based on those that are successful (interesting) in the other country-level forums. This central forum facilitates discussions taking place between citizens of the three Balkan countries and enable English-speaking emigrants (including second generation) to join in.

Each Western Balkans news agency is responsible for its own country-level forum with the appropriate news agency's journalists providing initial content and ongoing management. Successful discussions in these systems are used as the basis for discussions in the central English-language forum.

---

[5] <http://www.web-dep.eu/>.
[6] FP6-045003-WEB.DEP.
[7] <http://www.ata.gov.al/web-dep>.
[8] <http://www.web-dep.mia.com.mk/MIA>.
[9] <http://web-dep.tanjug.rs/default.aspx?page=home>.
[10] <http://central.web-dep.eu>.

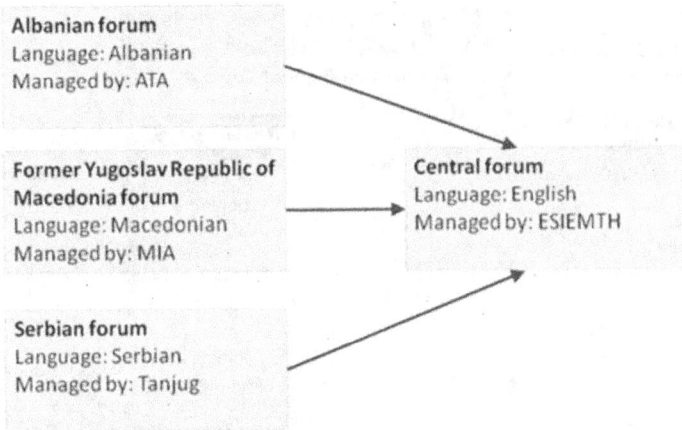

Figure 1. Forum installations.

eParticipation Operational Model

As the basic idea of the system is to host debates based on news provided by the news agencies, the journalists initiate the different topics that appear in the system based on news stories that appear on the front-page of each news agency website. The news agencies have appointed journalists to start discussions and provide supportive information. There are also mechanisms for providing citizens with opportunities to suggest discussion topics to journalists/moderators. The system is pre-moderated in order to avoid conflicts that may result in inappropriate use of it, and in this context every posting must be approved by a moderator (usually a journalist appointed by the corresponding news agency) before it is visible to everyone who visits the portal.

The eParticipation mechanisms used consist of two interactive tools: discussion and polling. Each discussion/poll combination should be based on a specific topic and be accompanied by supportive information. Space is provided for feedback (e.g. from government representatives) about the influence of these discussions. Journalists should collate and post supportive information and pursue and post feedback. The whole eParticipation operational model is shown in Figure 2.

Registered users are able to post their thoughts on the current topics. Each discussion (following a 'blog' format) is steered (facilitated) by the journalist who has initiated the topic, that is, the journalist is able to comment on the discussion progress, to identify other important themes that users suggest during the discussion and provide links between discussions and to relevant news items. Journalists may also begin new discussions based on issues which arise.

As the discussion progresses, the journalist is able to set up simple polls for each discussion. Those polls are focused on the different arguments that may spring out of the discussion procedure. Citizens need to be registered to vote in these e-polls.

Each discussion has a defined life cycle used for encouraging citizen involvement and for circulating the discussion results to the responsible stakeholders. Journalists set various time limits for the discussion and for the

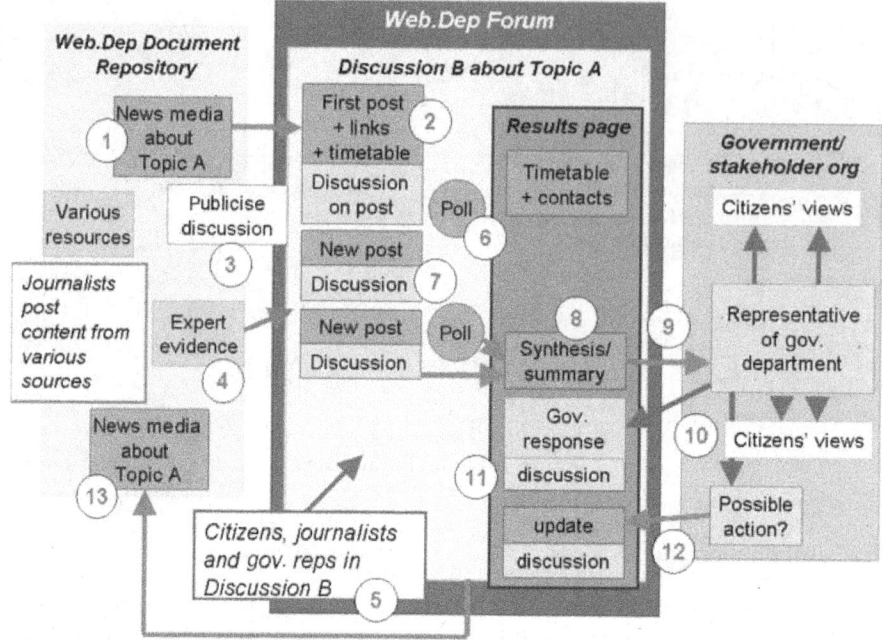

Figure 2. The eParticipation operational model.

polls in order that all stakeholders understand the shared agenda and to facilitate the delivery to the government decision-makers of the opinion of the citizens.

eParticipation Systems Evaluation Methodology

The methodology of eParticipation evaluation is still an open issue, and there is not a standard and widely accepted and used method for this purpose.[11,12] As depicted in Figure 3, an eParticipation system should satisfy multiple needs in order to be successful. These needs can be separated in two different categories, the IT driven category and 'political' or 'decision-making' driven category, which need to be satisfied both in a coordinated manner in order to deliver high-quality ICT-based decision support services to the citizens and governments.[13] The methodology we used for evaluating an eParticipation initiative combines these two perspectives, the former originating from information systems research and the latter from political sciences research; so it is implemented through two straightforward questionnaires addressing the actual users of the platform and aiming at capturing these two important dimensions of eDemocracy systems: the user perception of the usability and of the impact of the system to his/her

---

[11] A. Macintosh and A. Whyte, 'Towards an evaluation framework for eParticipation', *Workshop on Frameworks and Methods for Evaluating eParticipation*, Institute for Information Management, Bremen, Germany, 12 October 2007.

[12] E. Loukis and A. Xenakis, 'A framework for evaluating e-participation in the legislation development process', *EGOV 2008 International Conference*, Torino, Italy, 31 August–5 September 2008.

[13] Ari-Veikko Anttiroiko, 'Building strong e-democracy: the role of technology in developing democracy for the information age', *Communications of the ACM Archive*, 46(9), 2003, pp. 121–128.

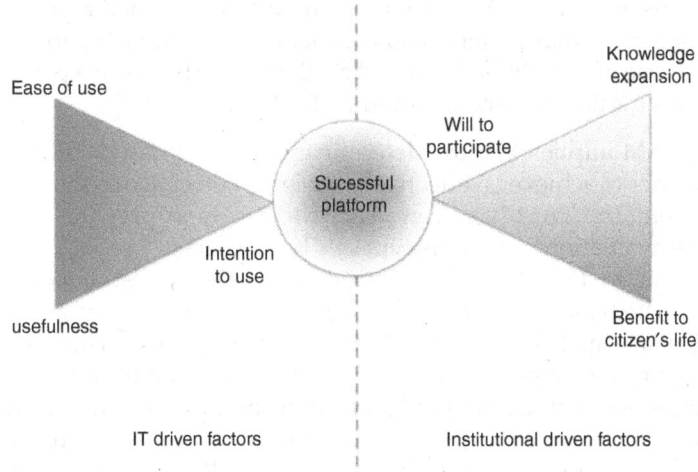

Figure 3. Success factors in eParticipation systems.

knowledge on the discussed topics, political behaviour, government decisions and benefits from them for citizens.

In this context and in order to evaluate the degree of success of an eParticipation platform amongst its users, one has to investigate both the aforementioned categories/perspectives, resulting in recommendations or guidelines that will strongly connect the aspects of system usability, in terms of user friendliness and straightforward functionalities, with those of the expected impact from the use of the system, in terms of increasing citizens' participation in the government decision-making progress and of making the public opinion heard and considered by the public decision-makers.

The proposed methodology, following this assumption, introduces an extended Technology Acceptance Model (TAM) for evaluating the system from the user's acceptance point of view, which is operationalized through a corresponding TAM Questionnaire, and a Political Evaluation Questionnaire, targeted to issues of eDemocracy and eParticipation.

TAM is an information systems theory that models how users come to accept and use a technology. It is one of the most influential extensions of Ajzen and Fishbein's theory of reasoned action (TRA)[14,15] and was developed by Davis et al.[16,17]

The model suggests that when users are presented with an ICT system, the two basic determinant factors that mainly influence its acceptance are:[18]

---

[14] I. Ajzen and M. Fishbein, *Belief, Attitude, Intention, and Behavior: An Introduction to Theory and Research*, Addison-Wesley, Reading, MA, 1975.

[15] I. Ajzen and M. Fishbein, *Understanding Attitudes and Predicting Social Behavior*, Prentice Hall, Englewood Cliffs, NJ, 1980.

[16] F. D. Davis, R. P. Bagozzi and P. R. Warshaw, 'User acceptance of computer technology: a comparison of two theoretical models', *Management Science*, 35, 1989, pp. 982–1003.

[17] F. D. Davis, R. P. Bagozzi and P. R. Warshaw, 'Development and test of a theory of technological learning and usage', *Human Relations*, 45(7), 1992, pp. 660–686.

[18] F. Makedon, S. Zhang, J. Ford, Z. Le and E. Loukis, 'Providing recommendations in an open collaboration system', *11th Panhellenic Conference on Informatics*, Patras, Greece, 18–20 May 2007.

- Perceived usefulness (PU), defined as 'the degree to which a person believes that using a particular system would enhance his or her job performance'.
- Perceived ease of use (PEOU), defined as 'the degree to which a person believes that using a particular system would be free from effort'.[19]

Practically, TAM implies that the determinants of the PU and PEOU should be focused in order to achieve an effective and highly correlated to the actual system use evaluation. The TAM has been used extensively in previous research as a basis for the evaluation of various types of ICT systems.[20]

In addition to the TAM Questionnaire, another questionnaire has been constructed which aims to evaluate the way the users see the system in terms of promoting eParticipation and eDemocracy in their region. This questionnaire aims to capture the offerings of such a system to a community by collecting answers on issues such as the potential extension of knowledge in the field of politics and decision-making, the promotion of the citizens' will regarding their participation in public dialogue and their overall opinion on whether the implemented systems generate benefits for their lives. All the statistical analyses of the data collected using these two questionnaires were performed using SPSS 16.0.

Applying a Technology Acceptance Model on the System

TAM was implemented through online questionnaires linked to the system instances and also paper questionnaires. Data, from both online and paper questionnaires, were processed together to evaluate the technology acceptance of the system.

The main steps that were followed for this evaluation were the following:

(a) Design of the questionnaire, addressing all the factors discussed above.
(b) Establishment of different research hypotheses providing the relations between the different factors/constructs of the model, in order to investigate the main determinants of user's acceptance.
(c) Distribution of the questionnaire and data collection.
(d) Data processing and testing of the hypotheses.

The different factors/constructs of the TAM we used in this study are the following:

- Perceived Usefulness
- Perceived Ease of Use
- Intention to Use
- External Factors.

This extended TAM we have used includes the basic TAM constructs, depicted in Figure 4, and also one new construct, namely, 'External Factors'. The aim of this extension is to identify the level of impact of relevant external factors (we have

---

[19] F. D. Davis, 'Perceived usefulness, perceived ease of use, and user acceptance of information technology', *MIS Quarterly*, 13(3), 1989, pp. 319–340.

[20] N. Karacapilidis, E. Loukis and S. Dimopoulos, 'Computer-supported G2G collaboration for public policy and decision-making', *The Journal of Enterprise Information Management*, 18(5), 2005, pp. 602–624.

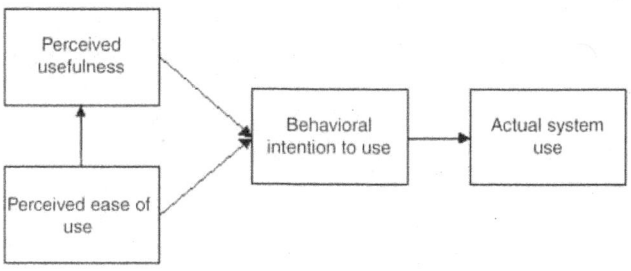

Figure 4. TAM approach.
Source: Davis *et al.* (1989), Venkatesh *et al.* (2003).

focused on prior experience, educational level and job/occupation relevance[21]) to Perceived Usefulness, Perceived Ease of Use and Intention to Use. This is of outmost importance when dealing with systems deployed in converging regions, as issues like digital divide, low Internet penetration and limited familiarization with technology become obstacles on the road towards the sustainable and beneficial implementation and operation of such a system.[22]

By analysing the users' inputs, it will become clearer whether factors such as prior experience with web tools, job/occupation relevance and educational level have a direct positive effect on the system's acceptance and operation in terms of the perceived usefulness, ease of use and intention to use it in the future. Following this approach, the extended TAM is presented in Figure 5, where the new construct named 'External Factors' has been added, including a set of information about the user's prior experience, occupation relevance and educational level. The TAM Questionnaire used can be found in the Appendix of this paper. We remark that for each of the above factors/constructs it includes several questions for achieving high levels of measurement reliability. The questionnaire was translated into the language of the users (country) of each system.

Research hypotheses The following research hypotheses were formulated in order to be tested based on users' responses based on the outcomes improvement scenarios can be built for maximizing the usability and the impact of the system:

- Hypothesis 1: Prior experience with similar technological tools and/or active citizenship will have a direct positive effect on system perceived usefulness.
- Hypothesis 2: Prior experience with similar technological tools and/or active citizenship will have a direct positive effect on system perceived ease of use.
- Hypothesis 3: Prior experience with similar technological tools and/or active citizenship will have a direct positive effect on intention to use the system.
- Hypothesis 4: Educational level will have a direct positive effect on system perceived usefulness.

---

[21] V. Vathanophas, N. Krittayaphongphun and C. Klomsiri, 'Technology acceptance of Internet toward e-Government initiative in naval finance department of Royal Thai Navy', *e-Government Workshop '06 (eGOV06)*, Brunel University, West London, 2006.

[22] Y. Charalabidis and E. Taylor-Smith, 'E-participation in converging European regions—workshop introduction presentation', *Proceedings of Workshop on 'E-participation in Converging European Regions', eGOV 2007 Conference*, Regensburg, Germany, 2007.

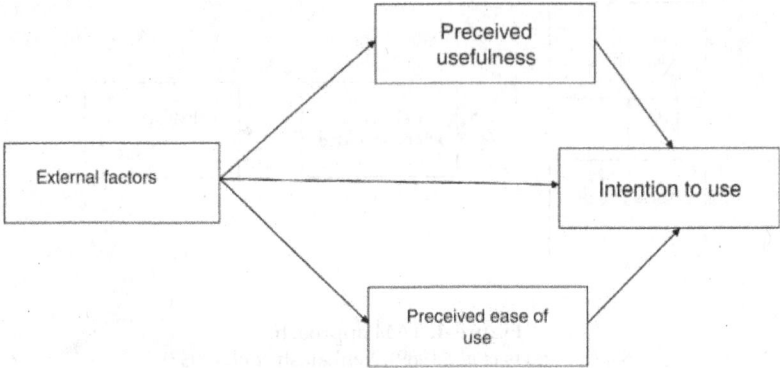

Figure 5. Extended TAM model used in this study.

- Hypothesis 5: Educational level will have a direct positive effect on system perceived ease of use.
- Hypothesis 6: Educational level will have a direct positive effect on intention to use the system.
- Hypothesis 7: Job/occupation relevance will have a direct positive effect on system perceived usefulness.
- Hypothesis 8: Job/occupation relevance will have a direct positive effect on intention to use the system.
- Hypothesis 9: Job/occupation relevance will have a direct positive effect on system perceived ease of use.
- Hypothesis 10: Perceived usefulness will have a direct positive effect on intention to use the system.
- Hypothesis 11: Perceived ease of use will have a direct positive effect on intention to use the system.

Political Evaluation Questionnaire

In addition to the TAM Questionnaire, another questionnaire, which aims to evaluate the way the users perceive from a political perspective the eParticipation system in terms of promoting eParticipation and eDemocracy in their region (whether they are the citizens who take part in the discussions or journalists), has been constructed. Questionnaires were translated into the language of the users (country) of each system. Each item/question is assessed in the same scale as the TAM Questionnaire.

Two open questions are also included, for capturing the users' opinions regarding the operation of the system and measuring its evolution over the remaining project period. This political questionnaire can be found in the Appendix of the paper.

Evaluation Results

Technology Acceptance Model Questionnaire Analysis

The analysis of the collected data consists of two parts. In the first part, the data for each one of the six constructs included in the TAM model will be processed

Table 1. Mean values of constructs

Construct	Mean value
Perceived usefulness	3.876
Perceived ease of use	3.899
Intention to use	3.960
Job/occupation training relevance	3.558
Prior experience	3.529
Educational level	3.947

independently (e.g. calculation of means and relative frequencies), extracting useful findings on the users (job/occupation, prior experience and educational level) and their attitude and satisfaction towards the system. In the second part of the TAM Questionnaire analysis multi-variety analyses are performed (e.g. calculation of correlations among the constructs) aiming at testing the 11 hypotheses.

Single construct analyses. In an attempt to extract some initial findings, the mean values for each construct were calculated and presented in Table 1 and Figure 6. The values presented were produced by calculating the mean value of the answers of the questions for each construct (Perceived Usefulness, Perceived Ease of Use, Intention to Use, Occupation/Training Relevance, Prior Experience and Educational Level) of the TAM Questionnaire.

Observations extracted from Table 1 are:

- The educational level of the user lies on 'Degree or higher training'.
- Perceived Usefulness, Perceived Ease of Use and Intention of Use are positive (lying on 'maybe yes' level which means 'Good').
- Users' occupation relation to IT technology and decision-making process and prior experience to discussion systems are slightly above the mean value of 3 which corresponds to 'yes and no' level ('Medium').

A deeper analysis for Perceived Usefulness, Perceived Ease of Use and Intention to Use, leads to a more consolidated view of these three fundamental constructs.

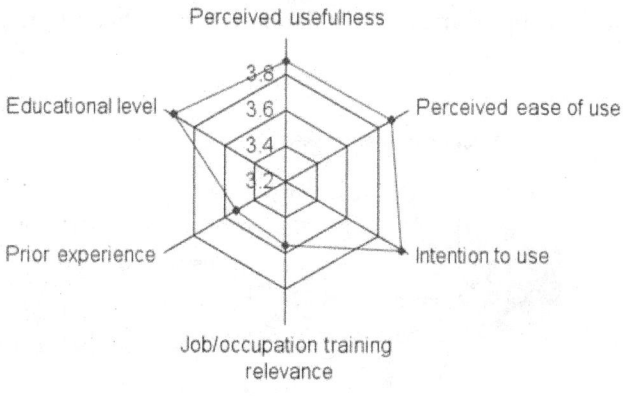

Figure 6. Construct mean values.

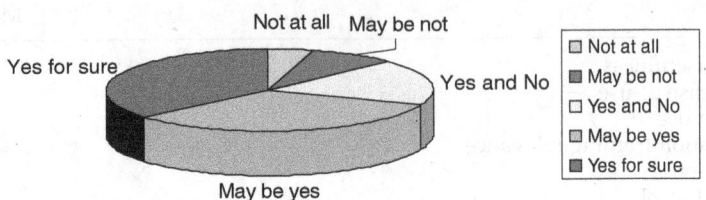

Figure 7. Response distribution on perceived usefulness.

The analysis includes the responses distribution for each one of these constructs. Figure 7 presents the responses distribution in the questions that are grouped under the 'Perceived Usefulness' of the questionnaire.

Figure 7 implies that a majority of users (72 per cent for 'maybe yes' and 'yes') believe in the usefulness of the system. The distribution of responses is similar for the perceived ease of use, shown in Figure 8, in which affirmative responses towards ease of use constitute the majority of 68 per cent ('maybe yes' and 'yes' responses).

Concerning Intention to Use, the positive trend of the users is even clearer while the negative answers are completely missing. This is depicted in Figure 8 which presents the distribution of the mean responses to the questions under the 'Perceived Ease of Use' category. Last but not least, Figure 9 presents the distribution of the average responses to the 'Intention to Use' category questions.

The initial findings reveal a positive attitude towards the eParticipation system by the users, with respect to usefulness, ease of use and also their intention to use it in the future. But in order to further elaborate the TAM and test the 11 research hypotheses about the effects of Occupation, Prior Experience and Education on Perceived Usefulness, Perceived Ease of Use and Intention to Use, and also the effects of Perceived Usefulness and Perceived Ease of Use on Intention to Use, a multi-variety statistical analysis should be performed in order to extract the correlations among these constructs. In this direction in the following section, the internal consistency and reliability of collected data are tested and then an attempt of approaching a correlation model for the constructs will be presented, using Pearson's correlation coefficients and linear regression technique.

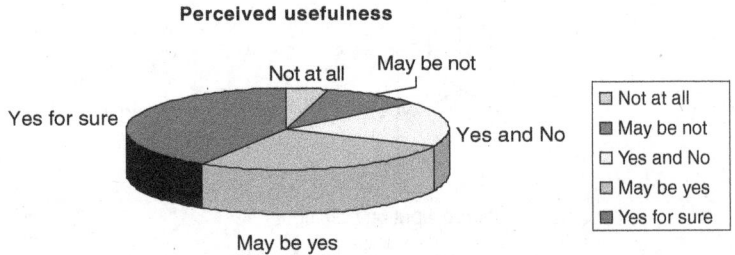

Figure 8. Response distribution on perceived ease of use.

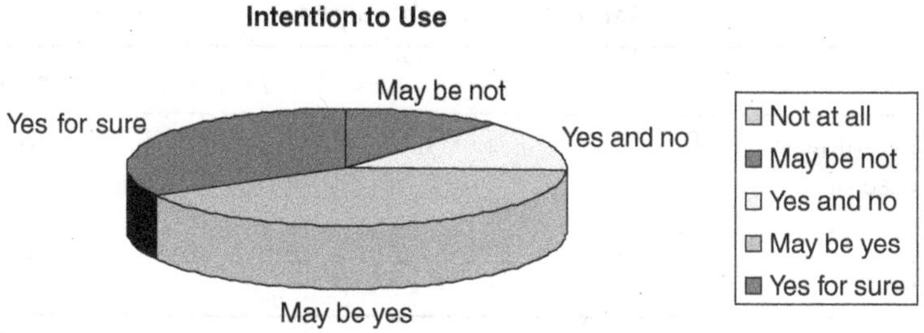

Intention to Use

Figure 9. Response distribution on intention to use.

Technology acceptability analysis—TAM implementation According to the pertinent statistical literature for each measurement taken, the observed score is made up of the true score and an error, the reliability coefficient (or Cronbach's alpha) is constructed by creating a ratio of the true score to the observed score, or in other words,[23] a ratio of the true score variance to the total variance, as part of it is due to error. In a completely reliable measurement the error is minimized to zero, so the ratio of true score to the observed one approaches 1.

TAM Questionnaire data was processed for each construct through SPSS 16.0, in order to extract its Cronbach's alpha value. The results are shown in Table 2; we can see that its values were satisfactory for all the constructs (exceeding the lowest acceptable value of 0.7 proposed by the pertinent statistical literature).

As the reliability is satisfactory, our next step was the attempt of extraction of the correlations among the constructs included in the 11 hypotheses of the TAM model. Correlation measures the association between two variables. A number of different coefficients are used for different situations. One of the most popular ones is the Pearson product–moment correlation coefficient, which is obtained by dividing the covariance of the two variables by the product of their standard deviations. In Table 3, the gathered data from the questionnaires was processed in order to extract the Pearson's correlations between the constructs.

We remark that none of the examined three external factors (relevant occupation, prior experience, education) has a statistically significant correlation with any of the three basic TAM constructs (usefulness, ease of use, intention to use). This indicates that the positive perceptions of the users do not vary significantly and are homogeneous across education, prior experience and occupation relevance groups; at the same time this shows that the system did not require special skills or experience from its users. On the contrary we remark that the three basic TAM constructs of Perceived Usefulness, Perceived Ease of Use and Intention to Use correlate each other strongly and positively; both the Perceived Usefulness and the Perceived Ease of Use seem to have a large effect on the Intension to Use, with the former being a stronger determinant of future intension to use eParticipation systems than the latter.

From the above correlations it is concluded that Hypotheses 1–9 are not supported, while Hypotheses 10 and 11 are supported, as shown in Table 4.

---

[23] J. P. Weir, 'Quantifying test–retest reliability using the intra-class correlation coefficient and the SEM', *The Journal of Strength and Conditioning Research*, 19, 2005, pp. 231–240.

Table 2. Cronbach's alpha

	Cronbach's alpha
Perceived usefulness	0.745
Perceived ease of use	0.779
Intention to use	0.779
Occupation	0.659
Prior experience	0.538

Political Evaluation Questionnaire Results

Overview. Overall, the responses gathered in the eParticipation Political Evaluation Questionnaires leaned more towards a positive view of the systems, with all the questions gaining more 'maybe yes' and 'yes for sure' answers, than 'not at all' or 'maybe not' answers. It should be mentioned that questions which directly concerned personal experiences of the users from the systems had a less positive response and a larger share of neutral ('yes and no') answers. This may be due to respondents placing a higher value on e-participation as an institutional intervention in general than on this specific instance/pilot. The results from processing these questionnaires are presented in detail in the Appendix in three categories based on the focus of the question:

(1) Effect on the person using the system.
(2) Impact of the systems on the political life.
(3) Attitudes towards e-participation.

For each question the results are divided into:

- results from responses from users of the ATA system,
- results from responses from users of the MIA system,
- plus total results from all responses, made up of these two sets, plus one response for the Central system.

Effect on the person using the system. The effect of the system on individual users, both registered participants and other visitors, is an important outcome, as democratic cultures and spheres are built on the skills and preferences of individual people, as well as of organized groups. The attitudes investigated by the questionnaires concern attributes that we associate with healthy democracies and active citizenship.

Responses indicated that the majority of respondents perceive the system as having a positive impact on their knowledge on politics and also their interest in participating in government decision-making (both in the traditional ways and through electronic channels). However, there were considerable percentages of respondents with negative opinions about the above aspects of the system (with answers 'Not at All' and 'Maybe Not'), probably taking into account the inherent weaknesses and problems of the rather 'young' democratic institutions in these national contexts. The 24 per cent negative responses to the question 'Has your knowledge in politics and decision making increased using the system?' may indicate an area in which the system could be improved, or may indicate that the

Table 3. Correlations

		Perceived usefulness	Perceived ease of use	Intention to use	Occupation	Prior experience	Education
Perceived usefulness	Pearson correlation	1.000	0.671**	0.824**	0.164	−0.457	−0.077
	Sig. (2-tailed)		0.006	0.000	0.575	0.087	0.785
Perceived ease of use	Pearson correlation	0.671**	1.000	0.510*	0.098	−0.321	0.048
	Sig. (2-tailed)	0.006		0.036	0.717	0.209	0.856
Intention to use	Pearson correlation	0.824**	0.510*	1.000	0.113	0.311	−0.052
	Sig. (2-tailed)	0.000	0.036		0.678	0.224	0.844
Occupation	Pearson correlation	0.164	0.098	0.113	1.000	0.389	−0.025
	Sig. (2-tailed)	0.575	0.717	0.678		0.136	0.926
Prior experience	Pearson correlation	−0.457	−0.321	−0.311	0.389	1.000	0.385
	Sig. (2-tailed)	0.087	0.209	0.224	0.136		0.126
Education	Pearson correlation	−0.077	0.048	−0.052	−0.025	0.385	1.000
	Sig. (2-tailed)	0.785	0.856	0.844	0.926	0.126	

**Correlation is significant at the 0.01 level (2-tailed).
*Correlation is significant at the 0.05 level (2-tailed).

Table 4. Hypothesis support

Hypothesis	Result
Hypothesis 1: Prior experience with similar technological tools and active citizenship will have a direct positive effect on system perceived usefulness.	Not supported
Hypothesis 2: Prior experience with similar technological tools and active citizenship will have a direct positive effect on system perceived ease of use.	Not supported
Hypothesis 3: Prior experience with similar technological tools and active citizenship will have a direct positive effect on intention to use the system.	Not supported
Hypothesis 4: Educational level will have a direct positive effect on system perceived usefulness.	Not supported
Hypothesis 5: Educational level will have a direct positive effect on system perceived ease of use.	Not supported
Hypothesis 6: Educational level will have a direct positive effect on intention to use the system.	Not supported
Hypothesis 7: Job/occupation relevance will have a direct positive effect on system perceived usefulness.	Not supported
Hypothesis 8: Job/occupation relevance will have a direct positive effect on intention to use the system.	Not supported
Hypothesis 9: Job/occupation relevance will have a direct positive effect on system perceived ease of use.	Not supported
Hypothesis 10: Perceived usefulness will have a direct positive effect on intention to use the system.	Supported
Hypothesis 11: Perceived ease of use will have a direct positive effect on intention to use the system.	Supported

questionnaires were completed by people with a good knowledge of politics in general and the particular issues under discussion in particular. This would likely be the case if the respondents were largely journalists and relevant workshop participants (many of the relevant workshop participants were involved in politically aware groups (government or NGO) or were students of political studies at universities; it was hoped that the observed system would serve as a useful educational resource, as it could be further utilised until discussions completed their life cycle). A high level of political activity and awareness among respondents may also be responsible for the low positive response (39 per cent) in the question 'Are you more encouraged to participate in political issues after using the system?' as respondents may already consider their participation as relatively strong.

Impact of the eParticipation system on the political life. Respondents to questions which aim to assess people's views of the likely political impact of the system are positive, but not overly optimistic. In particular, the majority of respondents believe that such a system has the potential to contribute to highlighting certain issues (that otherwise would be neglected or would gather less interest by the government), to the solution of some political issues, to the improvement of cooperation between NGOs, governmental organizations, news agencies and parliaments, and in general to bridging the gaps between citizens and governments and improving democracy in the Western Balkans. However, where a very definite path from the system discussions to government action was implied, respondents were cautious. It should be noted that, at the time of this evaluation, none of the e-discussions had been closed or forwarded to government contacts. Thus, however, where the notion of other organizations was introduced in the question: 'Will the system improve cooperation between NGO, governmental organizations, news agencies and parliaments?' a very positive response of 82 per cent was given. This may be due to the affiliation of the respondents (e.g. news agency and NGO), who are more confident of a positive change in the cooperation among their own organizations and with government. This was a good response, as it implied a positive attitude to cooperation among these organizations and with government. It should be noted that MIA system respondents' (FYROM) answers to the question: 'How do you think the system contributes in improving democracy in the Western Balkans?' were noticeably more negative in comparison with the other two West Balkan countries participating in this project, reflecting their pessimistic views concerning developments in this area.

Attitudes towards e-participation. Replies on attitudes towards e-participation in general, without focusing on the technology tools of the particular system, were clearly in favour of the use of e-participation, with 95 per cent agreeing that 'decision making for certain political issues should have contribution from e-participation mechanisms' and no one disagreeing. Respondents also agreed that the actual outcomes of the systems had a positive influence on their willingness to be more active politically, especially if they felt that if the results of the e-discussions taking place in this system are taken into consideration in stakeholders' subsequent actions.

About the system. The final question of this questionnaire asked for suggested improvements in the whole system. Respondents suggested technical improvements, without any detail of what was desired, making it difficult to pass this on to the developers. Respondents were clearer about extending the subject matter of the discussions towards political issues and to extending the reach of the system through use of other media.

Conclusions, Future Research

Conclusions from the Evaluations of the Pilots

This paper described the organization of a series of successful eParticipation pilots in the Western Balkans (Albania, FYROM and Serbia), an area characterized by intensive national and international tensions and rather young and immature democratic institutions. Also, their evaluation is presented, based on a 'synthetic' methodology, combining perspectives from the information systems and the political science domains; it included assessment of the technological acceptance of the eParticipation system by the users (a traditional perspective of the information systems research) and also its contribution towards political objectives: participative government decision-making and political deliberation (a traditional perspective of the political sciences research). The conclusions of this evaluation were in general positive, and this advocates the potential of eParticipation ICT in such special and highly difficult contexts (with tensions, lack of trust, immature democratic institutions, etc.).

In particular, as concluded from the analysis, the responses in the TAM Questionnaire included a good level of belief in the usefulness and ease of use of the system, and most respondents expressed their intension to use such a system again in the future. Moreover, none of the examined three external factors (relevant occupation, prior experience, education) had a statistically significant correlation with any of the three basic TAM constructs (usefulness, ease of use, intention to use), a fact that indicates that the positive perceptions of the users do not vary significantly and are homogeneous across education, prior experience and occupation relevance groups. On the contrary the three basic TAM constructs of Perceived Usefulness, Perceived Ease of Use and Intention to Use correlate each other strongly and positively.

Furthermore, the responses to the Political Evaluation Questionnaire were also largely positive. Respondents felt that using the system would have positive effects in terms of increasing their interest in current political issues, and, to a smaller extent, their knowledge on them. Also, they felt that such eParticipation systems might have a positive impact on the local political life, and contribute to highlighting and addressing certain political issues, and also to the improvement of cooperation between NGOs, governmental organizations, news agencies and parliaments, and in general to bridging the gaps between citizens and governments. Furthermore, people were enthusiastic about eParticipation and its possible impacts on the Western Balkans. On the other hand, responses to the Political Evaluation Questionnaire indicated that the investigated system was not at that point of time regarded as an information resource much beyond the general knowledge of the users, plus there was some criticism of the implementation and the particular topics discussed.

Further Research

As eParticipation systems are constantly developing, and new more advanced functionalities are added to them, such as map interfaces,[24] it is necessary to investigate and evaluate the use of advanced ICT for supporting and enhancing public participation of wider citizens' groups on various topics in such special and highly difficult national contexts, characterized by tensions, lack of trust and democratic traditions, immature democratic institutions, etc. For this purpose it is necessary to develop and use more sophisticated and comprehensive evaluation methodologies, which can combine different perspectives and frameworks (e.g. from political and social sciences and from information systems research), use a variety of data sources (e.g. collected through quantitative and qualitative research, analysis of discussion trees, etc.) and also can capture the multiple impacts (both positive and negative) of such eParticipation systems at various levels (e.g. at the level of individual, social group, civil society, government organization, political system, etc.).

---

[24] E. Loukis and M. Wimmer, 'Analysing different models of structured electronic consultation on legislation under formation', *4th International Conference on Online Deliberation—OD 2010*, Leeds University Business School, Leeds, 30 June–2 July 2010.

Sotirios Koussouris holds a PhD Degree in Information Systems and Business Process Management, a Dipl. Eng. in Computer and Electrical Engineering and a MBA in Techno-Economic Systems. His research interests include process and data modelling, IT system design, interoperability structures and focus on topics like eGovernment, eBusiness Systems, Decision Support Systems and Operational Management.

Yannis Charalabidis is an Assistant Professor at the University of the Aegean. He is a Computer Engineer and holds a PhD in Information Systems Engineering from National Technical University of Athens (NTUA). He has been employed for eight years as an executive director in Singular IT Group, specializing in ERP applications in South Eastern Europe. Currently he is heading e-Government and e-Business Research in the Decision Support Systems Laboratory of NTUA, planning and coordinating high-level policy-making, research and pilot application projects for governments and administrations worldwide. He teaches e-Government Information Systems, Interoperability and Standardization, eParticipation and Government Transformation in NTUA and the University of the Aegean.

Loukas Kipenis has received a Diploma in Electrical & Computer Engineering from National Technical University of Athens and is currently a PhD candidate in the School of Electrical & Computer Engineering, National Technical University of Athens. His research interests include IT system design, interoperability structures and focus on topics like eParticipation and eGovernment Systems.

Dimitrios Askounis is an Associate Professor in the School of Electrical & Computer Engineering of the National Technical University of Athens (NTUA). He has been involved in numerous EU-funded IT research projects since 1988 (ESPRIT, BRITE-EURAM, FP5, FP6) in the areas of computer integrated manufacturing, enterprise resource planning, decision support, knowledge management, quality management, business and data modelling, e-business, etc.

Odetta Stavri is currently Head of Partnership and Marketing in Albanian Telegraphic Agency. Holder of a master's degree in Law from University of Tirana, she comes from a solid experience with investment and foreign companies. Ms Stavri is responsible for the international cooperation of ATA in the framework of News Agency Organizations and her interests focus on public relations and consulting.

Appendix

A.1. Technology Acceptance Model (TAM) Questionnaire

Each question of the questionnaire is evaluated on a scale of 1–5, as follows:

(1) Not at all
(2) Maybe not—at low levels
(3) Yes and no—medium
(4) Maybe yes—good
(5) Yes for sure—very good.

Below are the questions, grouped by the different constructs of the model.

Perceived usefulness

- Are the discussions encouraging you to find out more about specific issues?
- Are the discussions providing you with new knowledge on current issues?
- Are the system functions (discussion initiation suggestions, eParticipation mechanisms, discussion procedure, voting mechanisms) helpful for conducting discussions?
- Are more functions needed regarding the 'flow' of the discussion?
- Do discussions arrive at results which should be taken into account by governmental organizations?
- Do you think it is good to use the system for reporting and discussing issues?
- Overall, would you say that the tools and technologies used are appropriate for the topics discussed?
- Do you prefer other, non-digital ways of participating as a citizen rather than this system?

Perceived ease of use

- Did you find it easy to register for the system?
- Is system navigation easy?
- Is the appearance of the website user friendly?
- Is information provided (e.g. help/guidelines) useful in performing tasks of the system?
- Is the discussion layout easy to follow?
- Did you find it easy to learn to use the system?
- Do you think that most people would need some training in order to start using the system?

Intention to use
- Do you intend to visit again?
- Do you intend to comment in the discussions?
- Does this website offer you any benefits you would not have in traditional participation (in politics and civil life), which attract you to use it again?

External factors

Relevant skills (in terms of job/occupation/education/hobby)
- Is your job/occupation/training related to decision-making (dealing with public issues or issues related to the system's topics)?
- Is your job/occupation/training related to IT?
- Is your job/occupation/training related to one of the discussion topics?

Prior experience
- Rate yourself in terms of experience as an Internet user?
- Have you used discussion systems before (No—1, Once—2, Less than 10 times—3, Less than 50 times—4, More than 50 times—5)?
- Have you ever used the Internet (e.g. website or e-mail) to contact local/regional/national government (No—1, Once—2, Less than 5 times—3, Less than 10 times—4, More than 10 times—5)?

Educational level
- Your educational level: None—1, Primary—2, Secondary—3, Degree or higher training—4, Postgraduate qualification—5.

E-PARTICIPATION IN SOUTHERN EUROPE AND THE BALKANS

A.2. Political Evaluation Questionnaire

Table A2.

EFFECTS ON THE PERSON USING THE SYSTEM
Has your knowledge on politics and decision-making increased using the system?

	ATA	MIA	Total (ATA + MIA + Central)	Negative/positive
Not at all	9%	40%	18%	24% −
Maybe not	0%	0%	6%	
Yes and no	9%	40%	18%	
Maybe yes	45%	20%	35%	
Yes for sure	36%	0%	24%	59% +

Has your interest in politics and decision-making increased using the system?

	ATA	MIA	Total	−/+
Not at all	0%	20%	6%	6% −
Maybe not	0%	0%	0%	
Yes and no	0%	60%	24%	
Maybe yes	73%	20%	53%	71% +
Yes for sure	27%	0%	18%	

Do you think that the system has inspired you to be more politically active?

	ATA	MIA	Total	−/+
Not at all	9%	40%	18%	36% −
Maybe not	18%	20%	18%	
Yes and no	18%	40%	24%	
Maybe yes	36%	0%	29%	41% +
Yes for sure	18%	0%	12%	

Are you more likely to participate in online discussions on political issues since visiting the system?

	ATA	MIA	Total	−/+
Not at all	9%	0%	6%	12% −
Maybe not	0%	20%	6%	
Yes and no	18%	60%	29%	
Maybe yes	36%	20%	35%	59% +
Yes for sure	36%	0%	24%	

Are you more encouraged to participate in political issues after using the system?

	ATA	MIA	Total	−/+
Not at all	9%	17%	9%	13% −
Maybe not	0%	17%	4%	
Yes and no	36%	33%	26%	
Maybe yes	27%	33%	26%	39% +
Yes for sure	27%	0%	13%	

IMPACT OF THE SYSTEM ON THE POLITICAL LIFE
Do you think that the results of the discussions in the system have an impact in governments?

	ATA	MIA	Total	−/+
Not at all	0%	0%	0%	18% −

Table A2 continued

Maybe not	9%	40%	18%	
Yes and no	0%	60%	24%	
Maybe yes	73%	0%	47%	59% +
Yes for sure	18%	0%	12%	

Do you think that the results of the discussions in the system could contribute to the solution of some of the political issues discussed?

	ATA	MIA	Total	−/+
Not at all	0%	0%	0%	18% −
Maybe not	0%	50%	18%	
Yes and no	0%	33%	18%	
Maybe yes	80%	0%	47%	65% +
Yes for sure	20%	17%	18%	

Do you think the results of the discussions highlight certain issues that otherwise would be neglected or would gather less interest by the government?

	ATA	MIA	Total	−/+
Not at all	0%	0%	0%	18% −
Maybe not	9%	40%	18%	
Yes and no	18%	40%	29%	
Maybe yes	45%	20%	35%	53% +
Yes for sure	27%	0%	18%	

Will the system improve cooperation between NGOs, governmental organizations, news agencies and parliaments?

	ATA	MIA	Total	−/+
Not at all	0%	0%	0%	6% −
Maybe not	0%	20%	6%	
Yes and no	0%	40%	12%	
Maybe yes	55%	40%	47%	82% +
Yes for sure	45%	0%	35%	

Do you think the system bridges a gap between citizens and governments?

	ATA	MIA	Total	−/+
Not at all	0%	20%	6%	6% −
Maybe not	0%	0%	0%	
Yes and no	9%	80%	29%	
Maybe yes	27%	0%	24%	65% +
Yes for sure	64%	0%	41%	

How do you think the system contributes to improving democracy in the Western Balkans? (Open Question)
o They do not contribute at all...
o By allowing the citizens to comment on a certain issue, even though the decisions are in the hands of politicians and by enabling the citizens to be informed about the viewpoints of government officials
o They don't contribute, they are badly conceived
o Compared to similar projects carried out in the EU, one can see how and whether this system exerts any influence in FYROM
o Not at all for the time being
o Average

Table A2 *continued*

ATTITUDES TOWARDS E-PARTICIPATION

Are you more likely to participate more in political issues, if the discussion results of the system are taken into consideration while performing political actions towards the discussed issues?

	ATA	MIA	Total	−/+
Not at all	9%	0%	6%	6% −
Maybe not	0%	0%	0%	
Yes and no	18%	33%	11%	
Maybe yes	36%	17%	33%	72% +
Yes for sure	36%	50%	39%	

Do you think that decision-making for certain political issues should have a contribution from e-participation mechanisms?

	ATA	MIA	Total	−/+
Not at all	0%	0%	0%	0% −
Maybe not	0%	0%	0%	
Yes and no	9%	0%	6%	
Maybe yes	9%	67%	56%	95% +
Yes for sure	45%	33%	39%	

ABOUT THE SYSTEM

How would you like to see the system improved? (Open Question)
- To inform the public through TV and e-mails
- It should be improved technically, together with its contents. Don't the agencies know what spelling is and how to initiate a discussion?
- Technically and functionally, it should be more clear and easy to use
- Yes

Constructing and implementing e-participation tools in the Emilia Romagna Region: assemblages and sense-making

ANDREA RESCA

Introduction

In simple terms, government can be seen as the sum of public bodies in charge of: (a) providing services to citizens and companies; (b) planning and implementing policy; (c) organizing administrative processes, systems and human resources in order to realize policy and implement the needed services.[1] However, this definition does not take into consideration the fact that new actors are involved in the management of public resources. The term governance[2] is used to represent a situation where both planning and policy implementation, on the one hand, and service provision, on the other hand, pursue an active role for actors outside the public sector. The so-called public–private partnerships serve as examples in this proposal. The concept of 'good governance'[3] further contributes to this aspect, emphasizing the role played by an environment in which citizens share and influence the social, political and economic priorities.

Information and communication technology (ICT) is an additional factor of this scenario. E-government is the general term that defines the alliance between government and ICT.[4] The large majority of interventions in this field concern the above-mentioned points of planning, organizing and service provision.[5] The ICT systems both at the front office and the back office have been objects of significant investment, while a large number of applications have been introduced on the basis of enhancing efficiency.[6] This managerial perspective has significantly

---

[1] Claudio Ciborra, *Teams, Markets, and Systems: Business Innovation and Information Technology*, Cambridge University Press, Cambridge, 1993.

[2] Jan Kooiman, 'Social–political governance', *Public Management Review*, 1(1), 1999, pp. 67–92; UNDP, *Governance for Sustainable Human Development*, 1997, available at: <http://mirror.undp.org/magnet/policy/> (accessed 9 July 2010).

[3] Ibid.; Thomas G. Weiss, 'Governance, good governance and global governance: conceptual and actual challenges', *Third World Quarterly*, 21(5), 2000, pp. 795–814.

[4] Jane E. Fountain, *Building the Virtual State: Information Technology and Institutional Change*, Brookings Institution Press, Washington, DC, 2001; OECD, *The e-Government Imperative: Main Findings*, Policy Brief, Public Affairs Division, Public Affairs and Communications Directorate, OECD, 2003.

[5] Christine Bellamy, Ivan Horrocks and Jeff Webb, 'Community information systems: strengthening local democracy?', in Wim B. H. J. Van De Donk, Ignace Th. M. Snellen and P. W. Tops (eds), *Orwell in Athens: A Perspective on Informatization and Democracy*, IOS Press, Amsterdam, 1995; Antonio Cordella, 'E-government: towards the e-bureaucratic form?', *Journal of Information Technology*, 22(3), 2007, pp. 265–274.

[6] Douglas Holmes, *eGov: E-Business Strategies for Government*, Nicholas Brealey, London, 2001; Charles Leadbeater, *Living on Thin Air*, new edn, Penguin Books, London, 2000.

contributed to the introduction of ICT in the sphere of public administration.[7] Nevertheless, focusing on 'good governance' implies a diverse approach for developing e-government. Factors such as legitimacy, accountability, justice and citizen participation, integrate with the efficiency rationale introducing a wider role of ICT in the public sector.[8]

E-participation initiatives are typically seen within this perspective:[9] ICT is seen as an additional, promising instrument for improving citizens' social and political participation—therefore extending managerial effectiveness towards good governance.[10] At least in Italy, the context of the present study, e-participation is making its first steps and a series of experiments have been put in place.[11] One of them is the focus of this research study: under the name of Partecipa.Net, it consists of an assembly of an e-participation system from the Emilia Romagna Region, in collaboration with other Italian public administrations.[12]

Two parts compose the present work, connected to each other: the first part targets the analysis of the process that led to the creation of this e-participation system, whereas the second part includes the study of the actual implementation of this system in two specific cases. The reason of this twofold point of view is to outline the techno-institutional context in which Partecipa.Net emerged as well as the transformation of this context into a system that has been used in actual practice—in two situations where citizens have been called to express their opinions on specific issues.

The development of the Partecipa.Net system has been investigated from the concept of an assemblage.[13] This concept is beneficial due to the characteristics inherent in the institutional and technological aspects of the project. The system emerges through a temporary collaboration between a series of public administrations, on the one hand, and existing technological devices provided by the administrations concerned, on the other. Therefore, both technological and

---

[7] David Osborne and Ted Gaebler, *Reinventing Government: How the Entrepreneurial Spirit is Transforming the Public Sector*, Plume, New York, 1993.

[8] Sam Agere, *Promoting Good Governance: Principles, Practices and Perspectives*, Commonwealth Secretariat, London, 2000; Eva Poluha and Mona Rosendahl, *Contesting 'Good' Governance: Crosscultural Perspectives on Representation, Accountability and Public Space*, Routledge, London, 2002.

[9] Damian Tambini, 'New media and democracy: the civic networking movement', *New Media Society*, 1(3), 1999, pp. 305–329; Andrew Chadwick, *Internet Politics: States, Citizens, and New Communication Technologies*, Oxford University Press, Oxford, 2006; Ann Macintosh, 'Characterizing e-participation in policy-making', in *Proceedings of the Thirty-Seventh Annual Hawaii International Conference on System Sciences (HICSS-37)*, Big Island, Hawaii, 2004.

[10] Bruce E. Tonn, Persides Zambrano and Sheila Moore, 'Community networks or networked communities?', *Social Science Computer Review*, 19(3), 2001, pp. 201–212; Claudio Ciborra and Diego D. Navarra, 'Good governance, development theory, and aid policy: risks and challenges of e-government in Jordan', *Information Technology for Development*, 11(2), 2005, pp. 141–159.

[11] Sara Bentivegna, 'Rethinking politics in the world of ICTs', *European Journal of Communication*, 21(3), 2006, pp. 345–356; Anna Carola Freschi and Vittorio Mete, 'The political meanings of institutional deliberative experiments. Findings on the Italian case', *Sociologica*, 3(2/3), 2009, <http://www.sociologica.mulino.it/doi/10.2383/31358> (accessed 9 July 2010); Davide Calenda and Lorenzo Mosca, 'The political use of the internet: some insights from two surveys of Italian students', *Information, Communication & Society*, 10(1), 2007, pp. 29–47.

[12] <www.partecipa.net> (accessed 9 July 2010).

[13] Giovan Francesco Lanzara, 'Building digital institutions: ICT and the rise of assemblages in government', in Francesco Contini and Giovan Francesco Lanzara (eds), *ICT and Innovation in the Public Sector*, Palgrave Macmillan, Basingstoke, 2009.

institutional components have been composed in an ad hoc solution that is appropriately represented by a concept like assemblage.

The study of the Partecipa.Net system applications involved a varied itinerary. Here, Heidegger's work on the phenomenology of religious life[14] has been taken as point of reference outlining an understanding of reality based on sense of 'content' (objects, people, physical and temporal circumstances, etc.), sense of 'relation' (network of meanings and references among objects, people, physical and temporal circumstances, etc.) and sense of 'actualization' or 'enactment' (how sense of 'content' and sense of 'relation' have been acted out and made active). In this proposal, the applications of the e-participation system have been investigated focusing (1) on the style of mediation adopted by facilitators in charge of the system and its usages (2) on the characteristics and dynamics that took place in the participation activity, and (3) on the atmosphere experienced by the users—participating citizens. Aspects such as existential disposition, mood, affectedness and emotion were then introduced into the research.

In the following section the Partecipa.Net system is introduced and then, in the third section, the evolution of this system is analysed according to the concept of assemblage. Sense of 'content', sense of 'relation' and sense of 'actualization' or 'enactment' are presented in the fourth section and these concepts are applied for studying the introduction of Partecipa.Net in two case studies in the fifth section. Some considerations on the participation rate in these cases are outlined in the sixth section and conclusions follow.

The Partecipa.Net System

In Italy, the diffusion of e-democracy is strictly related to public advice of the Italian Ministry for Technological Innovation that co-funded 56 projects in this field all over the country.[15] E-participation is considered an aspect of e-democracy and represents the whole of the technological and methodological instruments used to provide a further factor for rendering citizens' participation possible. In this regard, the Internet and other innovative channels constitute a possibility for transforming institutional and political communication, through two-way communication based on digital means, to support collaborative decision-making processes.

Partecipa.Net is a direct result of this initiative of the Italian government. It is an e-participation system envisaged by a consortium led by the Emilia Romagna Region in order to spread e-participation practices on its territory. It came to light in 2005, supported by the above-mentioned funds and by the Ministry of Innovation, the coordination and evaluation role played by CNIPA (National Centre for ICT in the Public Administrations) and the support of 21 local governments and 9 social associations. At the basis of this e-participation system there are two software applications: UNOX1 and Demos. UNOX1, a communication multi-channel system, has been developed by the Municipality of Modena whereas Demos, an electronic discussion forum, by the Municipality

---

[14] Martin Heidegger, *The Phenomenology of Religious Life*, Indiana University Press, Bloomington, IN, 2004.

[15] CNIPA, 'Linee Guida per la promozione della cittadinanza digitale: E-Democracy', 2004, <http://www.cnipa.gov.it/site/_files/e-democracyLG.pdf> (accessed 20 July 2010).

of Bologna. These two main applications have been integrated in a single system for enabling citizens' participation.

To investigate in further detail the Partecipa.Net system, it is useful to subdivide it into electronic identification, back office and front office.[16] Partecipa.Base is the software module dedicated to system access—username and password are required to login. So, every user has to register his/her name (also a nickname is allowed) to the Partecipa.Net portal indicating also an e-mail address in order to complete the registration procedure. Once this procedure is terminated, access to Partecipa.Net functionalities is available.

These functionalities are based on back office technologies and a database of users' profiles constitutes an important element among them as it enables the provision of services according to users' selected options. The FAQ (Frequently Asked Questions) engine is another back office element and a CMS (Content Management System) makes possible the organization of contents in a variety of formats (doc, txt, pdf, ppt, jpg, etc.). An open source GPL (General Public Licence) covers all Partecipa.Net system software components, in order to allow code reuse by other public administrations.

During the evolution of the system, the borders between electronic identification, front office and back office are becoming continuously more traversable, as new functions are introduced:

- Partecipa.Base, managing users' profiles, makes possible the organization of thematic newsletters and their forwarding to citizens that became subscribers during the registration phase.
- The Frequently Asked Questions (FAQ) function goes over back office borders as well: users have access to the Partecipa.Ask module, offering the possibility to submit questions to experts in a specific field.
- Partecipa.Poll is the module supporting surveys about issues at stake, also enabling electronic voting processes.
- The Partecipa.Forum module supports electronic forum and open debate activities. This module allows for interactions and discussion among enrolled citizens, moderator interventions and full-text search over the contents of the system.
- In order to facilitate discussion, Partecipa.Biblio, a virtual multimedia library is available.

The Partecipa.Net system is the final result of a project that had at its basis funds available from the Italian Ministry for Technological Innovation, this funding being the spark that put into motion the local administration. At this point, the Emilia Romagna Region summoned up local governments (municipalities and provinces) that could be interested in the e-democracy field. At first, the Regional Assembly, three municipalities, an association of municipalities and two provinces answered positively, then later the number of local government organizations participating reached 21.

The reasons that led these institutions to be part of the Partecipa.Net project are diverse. In some cases there is the motivation to upgrade software applications already available; in other cases the spur came from the provision of a regional law

---

[16] Lisa Viola Rossi, 'Un caso di e-democracy nel Comune di Ferrara: il progetto "Partecipa FERRARA"', Thesis, Università degli Studi di Ferrara, 2007.

that calls upon a wider involvement of citizens in democratic processes. Personal interests of local governors to experiment with e-democracy solutions is another usual cause. All these actors gathered in a working group that developed the project. The constitution of this group has been considered a success, not only because it succeeded in accomplishing the Partecipa.Net project requirements and deliverables, but also because it transformed itself into a platform with knowledge, relations and resources for developing other similar projects.

Partecipa.Net: An Assemblage?

After describing the main components of the system, it is now time to focus on the modalities through which Partecipa.Net has taken shape. The question at stake concerns the possibility of proposing a concept able to represent the sequence of events that led to the establishment of Partecipa.Net. A concept that both describes the characteristics of this e-participation system and how it can evolve. The notion of assemblage is considered useful in this direction. Even though it has been introduced by several authors,[17] Lanzara's definition is taken into account:

> *Assemblages result from the encounter and the multiple mediations between large ICT systems and the existing institutional frameworks and codes of the society. They are made up of heterogeneous components displaying multiple logics which cannot be easily reduced to one another. Hence, assemblages are not 'hybrid' entities, but rather 'composites'— collection of components, which tend to maintain their specificities.*[18]

It is supposed that these few lines succeed to illustrate rather well what effectively happened in the Partecipa.Net project. UNOX1 and Demos are the two ICT systems at the basis of this project, the Ministry for Technological Innovation, CNIPA, the Emilia Romagna Region and other local governments represent the institutional framework and the necessity to improve the quality of social and political participation can be seen as an aspect in the code of the society. What is emphasized by the concept of assemblage is that all these elements do not transform themselves into a new entity. On the contrary, UNOX1 and Demos are still there as other public bodies involved in the project. Therefore, assemblages are loosely structured and its components, even though they evolve continuously, maintain their autonomy in a situation in which boundaries and linkages tend to shift and drift. This means that assemblages are always ad hoc and change continuously. Changes take place at different speed according to the different elements involved given that each component has its own time of evolution. Therefore, in these conditions, equilibriums are always unstable. Lanzara[19] identifies a series of features that characterize assemblages:

- The presence of multiple actors and authority structures of which none of them exercises full control on the project whereas each is in charge only of a part of it

---

[17] Robert Cooper, 'Assemblage notes', in Robert Chia (ed.), *Organized Worlds: Essays in Technology and Organisation with Robert Cooper*, Routledge, London, 1998; Aihwa Ong and Stephen J. Collier, 'Global assemblages, anthropological problems', in Aihwa Ong and Stephen J. Collier (eds), *Global Assemblages: Technology, Politics, and Ethics as Anthropological Problems*, Blackwell, Oxford, 2005.

[18] Lanzara, op. cit., p. 13.

[19] Lanzara, op. cit.

(i.e. CNIPA, Emilia Romagna Region and other local governments).
- Institutional sponsors and project champions emerge. That is, some actors acquire a leading role promoting innovation and taking responsibility of coordination (i.e. Emilia Romagna Region).
- Episodes, discontinuous activities and situated interventions are seen as further characteristics of assemblages. In other words, activities are not regular (the business as usual of the different components has to go on) but based on specific agreements among actors involved in a specific commitment (i.e. in Partecipa.Net, working groups were autonomous and slightly coordinated by the Emilia Romagna Region).
- Adapting, repairing and redesign of available components consist of the fact that design activities tend to be focused on components already in place that need to be tailored to a new context. At the basis of this way of doing, there are the following questions: what is possible to do with what is already available? What functionalities can be added to present systems in order to pursue our objectives? What kind of simplifications can be introduced in order to streamline existing procedures? (i.e. UNOX1 and Demos experienced this type of handling).
- Converting, linking and plumbing. They are related to the conversion and the following connection of components at place in order to build a more complex assemblage (i.e. UNOX1 and Demos have been re-adapted and connected to each other).
- Redesigning administrative routines, interfaces and jurisdictions is enabled by the different systems that now are connected to each other. Procedures involved in separated domains are now linked leading to a new way of doing things (i.e. the combination of UNOX1 (a system for informing citizens about social and institutional life of the Municipality of Modena) and Demos (an electronic forum) as the basis of participation activities electronically supported).
- Characteristics of the installed base (pre-existing technical and institutional materials) can be more or less obtrusive or enabling. The possibility to introduce gateways, the level of re-combinability and the degree of modularity contribute to the taking shape of new assemblages (i.e. UNOX1 faces technical problems in its adoption and Demos functionalities support a specific decision-making process that can be in contrast with normal procedures in offline situations).

To conclude, Lanzara[20] suggests that assemblages can be evaluated according to three main perspectives: technical compatibility, functional compatibility and institutional compatibility. Technical compatibility refers to standards, modularity, interfaces, protocols, etc. At present, Partecipa.Net technical compatibility is still at stake. Several pilot projects have already been put into practice and two of them will be taken into consideration in the following sections. Nevertheless, Partecipa.Forum is considered too rigid and outdated from a technical point of view, interoperability issues have continued to emerge among the different components and security standards of Partecipa.Net do not match Emilia Romagna Region requirements, for example. Concerning functional

---

[20] Ibid.

compatibility, the question related to the consonance between technological components and social and institutional components (i.e. does Partecipa.Net effectively support social–political participation?) has been raised as well. Is Partecipa.Forum the most appropriate tool as it is based on a specific method of participation named Delphi that is considered too complex to be implemented? Only institutional compatibility (satisfactory forms of collaborations among agencies and organizations involved in assemblages due to a shared language, mutual understanding and accountability) does not seem to be called into question. All of this means that the future of Partecipa.Net is uncertain and it is not excluded that it will be discharged even though, most probably, as an assemblage, it will continue to transform itself taking other shapes.

The Sense of 'Content', 'Relation', 'Actualization' or 'Enactment': A Way to Emphasize Ontology in E-participation Research

Research activity, at least in the realm of social science, tends to concentrate on epistemology (how we know, what we know and how knowledge can be acquired on the entities being examined) rather than ontology (the study of being, of what exists and of what is thinkable). Every research paper dedicates a portion of it to epistemology. Conversely, ontology is often neglected or considered tacitly. Among the objectives of this work, there is that one to focus on ontology. That is, to emphasize the range of what is the object of investigation trying, at the same time, to take into consideration further aspects of reality. An opportunity in this respect is provided by Heidegger's work on the phenomenology of religious life.[21] Here, he suggests a comprehension and an investigation of reality (ontology) based on sense of 'content', sense of 'relation' and sense of 'actualization' or 'enactment'.

Sense of 'content' refers to entities present in a situation: objects, people, physical and temporal circumstances, etc. It delineates a facet of existence or reality that emphasizes the objectivity and materiality of entities and also what is experienced. It highlights the objective aspect and the characteristics of the 'content' under examination. To be more precise on this point, it is worthwhile to turn to Ciborra's work[22] on the characteristics of information infrastructures in Milan in which the same approach has been used. Here, sense of 'content' is represented by hardware, software, cables and wireless systems that have been installed in the city and, in addition to these systems, the usage rate of telephones and computer networks both in the private (citizens and companies) and public sectors. Even the concept of assemblage can be seen according to the lenses proposed by sense of 'content'. ICT systems, the existing institutional frameworks and codes of the society that are the main components of assemblages can be considered factors of such sense.

Sense of 'relation' refers to the network of meanings and references among entities of the same situation. It answers to the 'how' question rather than the 'what' question that typifies sense of 'content'. Therefore, how is 'content'

---

[21] Heidegger, op. cit.; John MacQuarrie, *Heidegger and Christianity: The Hensley Henson Lectures 1993–94*, Continuum International Publishing Group, New York, 1999.

[22] Claudio Ciborra, 'Note Fenomenologiche su Milano e le Reti', in Mauro Magatti (ed.), *Milano, nodo della rete globale: un itinerario di analisi e proposte*, Mondadori, Milano, 2005.

connected? That is, how are its components related to each other? In addition, how are these connections experienced? To answer these issues means to investigate relationships and references established within the sense of 'content'. Once more, Ciborra's work[23] can be of some help in analysing this sense as it is posed that it is not sufficient to focus on information related to the range and the characteristics of the city network and its usage rates are not sufficient to examine its role. The research inquiry should be broadened to include the social, political and business relationships of which these infrastructures are an integral part of and the modalities through which they are influenced. So, sense of 'relation' involves the investigation of courses of action and the capabilities required to set up relationships through what has been mentioned above as 'content' (i.e. hardware, software, etc.) within a territory and at a global level. This is seen as the fundamental way for understanding if and how this network is instrumental for Milan's development. In this case as well, the concept of assemblage is helpful for investigating sense of 'relation'. The fact that assemblages are made up of heterogeneous components displaying multiple logics, which cannot be easily reduced to one another, emphasizes this sense. The range of analysis is not only restricted to objective aspects of phenomena, here, meanings and references due to interactions among these aspects are investigated as well. This is to say that a dual perspective connotes concepts such as assemblage due to the possibility to throw light on both objective aspects and relational and dynamic aspects of phenomena.

Nevertheless, this kind of concept shows its limits when examining the stream of life in which phenomena are embedded. As far as it concerns objectifying descriptions and meanings related to phenomena, these instruments of analysis are considered appropriate but fall short if existential terms are taken into consideration. Sense of 'actualization' or enactment is the answer in respect of the ontological issue posed at the beginning of this paragraph. Here, the focus moves towards how 'content' and 'relation' have been enacted and made active. Precisely, the point is to grasp attitudes and the ways in which existence informs 'content' and 'relation' as sense is created through life's practices. However, to highlight life enactment prevents us in placing excessive importance on the objectification of 'content' and 'relation' which casts a shadow on their actualization and how existence is carried out through the senses of 'content' and 'relation'. In order to investigate Milan's information infrastructure 'in action', Ciborra[24] pointed towards the ethnographies in case studies where at the basis of these methods is the objective to investigate the valuable meanings and concrete experiences that such information infrastructures provide.

The ontological perspective proposed in this work is also emphasized by the analysis of the term 'enactment' proposed by Weick.[25] According to Weick's point of view, enactment acquires a diverse meaning in comparison with what has been proposed by Heidegger's work. Using Piaget[26] as another point of reference, the cognitive aspect rather than the existential one is at the centre of the

---

[23] Ibid.
[24] Ibid.
[25] Karl Weick, 'Enactment processes in organisations', in Barry M. Staw and Gerald R. Salancik (eds), *New Directions in Organisational Behavior*, St Claire Press, Chicago, 1977.
[26] Jean Piaget, *Play, Dreams and Imitation in Childhood*, Routledge and Kegan Paul, London, 1962.

discourse. Here the individual is seen as an entity that punctuates and activates the flow of experience, which is then transformed *'in a network of causal sequences or causal map'*.[27] In both perspectives the process of 'sense-making' is crucial, the latter being intended as the final result of a mental process in which local circumstances are detected and elaborated (based on inputs acquired in the context of which actions are taking place). Heidegger's perspective is far from emphasizing causal sequences as the engine of the sense-making process. Rather, it is the consequence of existential disposition, mood, affectedness and emotion. The sense-making process can only be represented in this way.

Sense of 'content', sense of 'relation' and sense of 'actualization' or 'enactment' add existential aspects to our comprehension of phenomena. Institutional and historical circumstances, for instance, continue to be fundamental to the understanding or the interpretation, nevertheless existential aspects, to some degree, add colour to the phenomena under investigation.

Furthermore, Heidegger's approach questions an instrument of research as theories. Sutton and Staw conceive them as 'stories about why acts, events, structure, and thoughts occur'.[28] But, for this reason, they are seen as obstacles in order to investigate reality and the sense-making process if, at the centre of this argument lies factual life experience.[29] Factual life experience is intended as something more than a cognitive experience and may not be interpreted through epistemological perspectives. Objects are transformed into a 'world' so that self-experiences and what is actually experienced are no longer separated. It is how individuals stand in relation to events in everyday life that is important. In factual life, subjects do not experience themselves in a series of acts and procedures. Rather, what the individual experiences is related to human emotions such as hurt, pain, happiness and joy.

E-participation and Sense-Making

Actual deliberation within the Partecipa.Net system was performed in two specific cases: 'gli orari della città' and 'per via Gallucci'. In the 'gli orari della città' case, the objective was to involve citizens of the Municipality of Modena, in order to reorganize opening hours of bars, shops, public offices and also public transportation timetables and, in this way, to render more welcoming the city. 'Per via Gallucci' represents an attempt to put under control conflicts aroused between via Gallucci residents, on the one hand, and customers and barkeepers of the same street, on the other hand, as via Gallucci is one of the more famous streets for its night spots in Modena.

The methodology used to investigate these two e-participation projects is in the circle of the case study research.[30] The research question at stake here is related to the meanings and the interpretations of participation which emerged in the two cases under examination. In order to follow this objective, Partecipa.Net facilitators have been interviewed. In fact, the functioning of this

---

[27] Weick, op. cit., p. 275.
[28] Robert Sutton and Barry Staw, 'What theory is not', *Administrative Science Quarterly*, 40(3), 1995, pp. 371–384.
[29] Heidegger, op. cit.
[30] Robert K. Yin, *Case Study Research: Design and Methods*, Sage, Thousand Oaks, CA, 2003.

e-participation tool requires a figure in charge both of possible technical problems encountered by users and of possible misunderstandings and conflicts aroused among participants in the use of Partecipa.Forum.

Study propositions or issue sub-questions are helpful in order to enrich the research question at stake enlightening more in detail the directions that this study pursued. Three sub-questions seem to be significant in this regard: the style of mediation or facilitation, the characteristics of participation and the atmosphere experienced by users.

Units of analysis represent a further step in this research design. Units of analysis in this case are 'gli orari della città' and 'per via Gallucci' facilitators. As it has been mentioned above, it is through their role that the research question and, of course, even sub-questions, have been examined. However, this role has been interpreted turning to the three 'worlds' proposed by Heidegger:[31] the 'surrounding world' (milieu), the 'communal world' and the 'self world'. Actually, the units of analysis are based on the overlapping of these three 'worlds'.

The final step concerns the interpretation of findings and then modalities that lead to meanings and understandings related to participation in 'gli orari della città' and 'per via Gallucci'. Even in this case, Heidegger's perspective proposed above has been taken as the main point of reference. This means that the investigation of sense of 'content', sense of 'relation' and sense of 'actualization' or 'enactment' constitute the main factors to examine the 'rationale' (verbum internum) of the introduction of the Partecipa.Net system in these two cases. Case similarities (users coming from the same context, the same technological system and similar subject of application) lead us to study them altogether rather than in their singularities.

The Style of Mediation: Meanings and Interpretations

The mission of the facilitator was not to be directly involved in what was going on in the forum or in other activities that supported participation. Rather, it was his/her responsibility to supervise activities in a detached way without influencing the substance of what was the object of discussion. Nevertheless, it was fundamental to play an active role leading debates and exchanges of ideas in what was considered relevant for the issues at stake. This was the reason why facilitators were trained, even though not in an exhaustive way, both in order to avoid problems of etiquette in the forum conduct and to guide discussions to support the creation of the so-called collective intelligence as it has been emphasized by one of the facilitators. Collective intelligence consists in identifying viable solutions in order to deal with issues at stake and all of this requires a series of activities related not only to the management of interactions but also to the support of appropriate information, contents, statistical data, etc. All these considerations emphasize sense of 'content' of mediation.

Sense of 'content' refers to entities present in a situation as objects, people, technology, values and cultures. Differently, sense of 'relation' refers to the network of meanings and references that emerged from relationships established by these entities. Therefore, the point now is to analyse the nature of connections that took place at the level of mediation. Technical problems, substantially, did not occur. In some cases, it has been necessary to support users at the authentication

---

[31] Heidegger, op. cit.

stage but this was all. A more active role by mediators was required when discussions turned out to be useless, not creative or not containing a proposal. This was mainly the case when objects of debate were not close to participants' needs. In those situations, it was necessary to revitalize interactions even though, sometimes, the role of leadership put at stake by facilitators was not considered sufficient. Probably, it would have been necessary to be more incisive in order to bring into question relevant issues that could not get into the debate only relying upon forum users' interventions. In this proposal, it is necessary to take into consideration the inexperience of the actors involved in the two projects. Furthermore, there was not an established background regarding modalities to manage the forum. In fact, it bears in mind that from the perspective of the Municipality, these projects were innovative. Actually, a new offline form of participation has recently been introduced. This also means that local administrators and local politicians were inexperienced in this respect and had no opportunity to develop a sufficient foundation in which to launch this type of decision-making process in the city government.

The objective, at this point, is to examine sense of 'actualization' or 'enactment' experienced in the course of mediation. That is, the wonder is how 'content' and 'relation' have been made active and in the stream of life by facilitators. The role of the facilitator has been lived in a rather distant and aloof way. The professional character prevailed rather than an approach closer to existing debates. The facilitators' lack of experience, at least in the case of managing e-participation projects, led to an attitude of cautiousness. They were concerned that excessively influencing the discussion and directing the decision-making process towards the pre-established aims of the Municipality could be harmful. The result was that users considered facilitators to perform a gatekeeper role, to supervise over forum activities. Indeed, a gentlemen's agreement occurred during the course of forum activities. Furthermore, facilitators were seen to be, in some way, representatives of the Municipality of Modena and not as neutral actors in charge of the supervision of online participation. So, it is possible to presume that the institutional role played by this local government brought about a kind of fear and also a suspicion amongst those users who influenced the nature of debates. On the facilitators' side, they perceived the sense of instability and hesitation that characterized the management of the projects and this contributed to determining their style of mediation. This style stressed the value of distance and supervision rather than any direct involvement in the discussion. Besides, it was not clear if, once specific results were reached, they would be taken into consideration for policy-making.

The Characteristics of Participation: Meanings and Interpretations

Even in this case, the analysis of the features of participation begins from the sense of 'content'. In this proposal, the themes of the electronic forum have been considered important. The level of interactions risks being sterile, fruitless and unable to attract a considerable number of participants in case they were not really close to citizens. The point that themes have been decided by the Municipality and not by citizens themselves has been considered an aspect that, in some way, influenced negatively the development of the 'gli orari della città' and 'per via Gallucci' projects. A further factor that outlines the what of participation is related to its size and measures taken in order to allure a large number of citizens. A traditional advertising campaign for explaining in detail the terms of the issues at stake to be faced through deliberative procedures was considered fundamental. Besides, information spread across existing electronic means as the Municipality mailing lists or to the UNOX1 services was used as well. In this regard, it is not an easy task to inform citizens about the possibility to participate actively in a decision-making process through the Internet. Municipality attitude in respect of the Partecipa.Net tool was not completely supportive, all potentialities of such a tool have not been taken into consideration and also their planning stage was not considered sufficient.

Concerning sense of 'relation', in both cases under examination it was possible to detect a learning process. That is, the modalities and also the quality of discussions improved considerably as time passed. Users developed a reciprocal understanding, evaluations on the objects of debate became continuously more accurate, and from that emerged constructive proposals that put into question the contents of the discussions in course. Nevertheless, it was not possible to say that at the end of the process a sort of community took shape. In the next section, the level of participation in the two projects will be examined and outlined. The data show that only a few dozen people had been active in the forum. This fact significantly influenced the nature of participation. A limited number of actors, who were mainly participants in the forum hampered the potential for a rich discussion and the emergence of diversified positions. This problem was exacerbated by the possibility of a dominant position emerging. This is precisely what occurred in one of the projects in question.

Members of a local council, representative of specific interests, decided to join the forum. However, even though their activities contributed significantly to enrich the level of discussions, their specific position was over-represented biasing the terms of the debate. This is one of the negative side effects enabled by e-participation tools.

Sense of 'actualization' or 'enactment' is investigated focusing both on Municipality and citizens' attitudes in respect of the 'gli orari della città' and 'per via Gallucci' projects. Citizens who decided to be involved in these two projects saw e-participation as a further instrument to have a say in the city government. Frustrations and also hostility toward the Municipality were perceptible due mainly to problems aroused in via Gallucci. Dissatisfactions that usually had no chance to be expressed in the public sphere found a new way to be channelled. Of course, the presence of prejudicial perspectives constituted an obstacle in the progress of participation. Furthermore, there was the question as to whether this new opportunity allowed a more incisive protest and also the possibility to make some proposals. Actually, some results have been reached and suggestions determined in the forum have been taken into consideration. Besides, as time passed, the hostile attitude reduced significantly and the level of discussion became more fruitful.

A sense of collaboration emerged, suggesting that an instrument like a forum can actually be instrumental in reconsidering certain convictions and beliefs and to delineate, possibly, new scenarios on specific issues.

The Municipality of Modena is not alien to this situation: tools like Partecipa.Net were seen as something new, a little strange, and marginal and not as a solution to be prioritized. Therefore, there has been the impression that the decision to adopt these tools was to pretend to be innovative and up to date. Italy, and particularly Emilia Romagna and the city of Modena have been subject to the rhetoric of participation. Local administrators and local politicians have been eager to introduce new forms of social and political participation, a fact that emphasizes the movement towards establishing a quality democracy.

At a national level, Emilia Romagna, specifically in the field related to the so-called good administration, is considered to be a region that makes considerable effort to be avant-garde in introducing innovative solutions to satisfy its citizens' needs. Nevertheless, innovation is risky and costly, as in the case of e-participation projects, insufficient knowledge was available regarding these deliberative procedures. This led to the perception of politicians not being in control of the situation. They were concerned about the consequences of such projects. How will the results of the deliberative procedures be taken into consideration? What level of participation can be considered sufficient in order to assess whether these results are valid and, then, representative of the general consensus? These are legitimate questions and only further analysis will clarify the appropriate modalities to proceed in this direction. For the time being, traditional ways to stimulate participation, like local assemblies, still seem preferred.

The Atmosphere Experienced by Users: Meanings and Interpretations

In order to take into consideration sense of 'content' related to users, let us start from their features. Age-wise there were not only young people: on the contrary, the majority were between 30 and 50 years old. The language style used suggested that many of them were professionals or highly educated and with a significant computer literacy level. This means that the young and the old range of the population were not importantly represented. In addition, participation was not anonymous. As it has already been mentioned, users' registration was required, even though it was possible to use nicknames rather than real ones.

Concerning sense of 'relation', it has to be mentioned that discussions have also reached high levels of significance. This outcome is not unexpected. Actual participants did not represent all society groups, but rather a specific segment—this fact contributing to the establishment of a relatively stable environment for debating. So, we are not in the range of chatting. Rather, there has been the impression that participants have been motivated and committed to their own points of view. There was a discernible shared awareness about the importance and the value of activities in course.

At least in one of the two cases, two categories of participants could be detected: those connected to the local council mentioned above and the rest. The former tended to focus only on the subject of direct interest whereas the latter touched on a far larger range of issues. These two categories influenced also sense of 'actualization' or 'enactment'. A sense of solidarity emerged in the local council group. The proverb 'united we stand, divided we fall' well represents the atmosphere shared by this group of people. Even though the depth of cohesion demonstrated by this group succeeded in characterizing the way in which to participate in and support a specific position. On the other hand, it created prejudices and preconceptions around other contributors regarding the participation of this group. In other words, participation dynamics were substantially predictable. The rest of the participants expressed a different attitude—the attitude of those men and women, who cordially but firmly exchanged ideas on the subjects at stake, did so without being influenced by a specific sense of belonging. Rather, they took very individual stances and expressed their own opinions freely.

The Rate of Participation in the Partecipa.Net Projects: An Analysis and Some Suggestions

The data relating to the proliferation of e-participation in the two cases, so far, under examination have not been presented. The idea at the basis of this decision was to approach this topic at the end of the paper in order to reflect and draw out some conclusions.

Data regarding 'gli orari della città' and 'per via Gallucci' are not easily comparable even though it is possible to draw out some points. Data in Table 1 point out that mailing list users (43,500 people) of UNOX1 services had been informed about the 'gli orari della città' project. At the same time, a conventional advertising campaign was launched giving the complete demographic of the citizens who would be targeted about the e-participation project. Web page hits indicate the number of hits that the Partecipa.Net system received—this amounted to 11,258 in contrast to 1216 hits recorded by the forum. Despite having over one thousand hits for the forum, only 88 comments had been recorded and only 117 questionnaires completed and submitted. The latter is related to the forum and was used to select subjects to be discussed through Partecipa.Poll.

Concerning 'per via Gallucci', data relating to the forum are not available and data relating to questionnaires are unrepresentative as they were only completed by a few dozen citizens. The number of citizens informed by this project was similar to the 'gli orari della città' project, as in this case, it had been run as an analogous campaign.

Clearly, this rate of participation is unsatisfactory. Furthermore, it is hard to have a discourse on e-participation when a narrow segment of the population actively takes part on an issue of public interest as in the case of 'per via Gallucci' or 'gli orari della città'. In addition, this is not only a problem concerning the Municipality of Modena. Data concerning other projects (i.e. the Municipality of Ferrara, see Table 2), always in the circle of Partecipa.Net, indicate a similar trend.

Table 1. Data related to the 'gli orari della città' project at the Modena Municipality

Mailing list users	43,500
Web page hits	11,258
Forum hits	1216
Number of comments on the forum	88
Filled questionnaires	117

Source: Comune di Modena.

Table 2. Data related to Forum Agorà (10 forums on main priorities of Ferrara citizens)

Web page hits (informative material)	5126
Forum hits	4403
Number of comments on the forum	261
Participants to the forum	36

Source: Comune di Ferrara.

Nevertheless, these projects should not have only been evaluated from such a negative perspective. New ideas emerged and inputs from participants led to interventions that were effectively put into practice. Local administrators started to be more familiar with tools such as Partecipa.Net and began to see and praise its potential. Quarrels and other unfortunate misunderstandings did not take place and even more hostile attitudes vanished as time passed. This is significant considering that offline practices of participation are usually characterized by high levels of contentiousness.

The role played by the local council in the e-participation projects promoted by the Municipality of Modena led to a further noteworthy consideration. Projects like Participa.Net clearly target citizens. However, participation is not only characterized by the individual level but also by the institutional/organizational level.[32] To participate and to be actively engaged in a process or act such as a decision-making process, for example, requires great personal commitment and an underlying belief that the process reflects the individual's own values.

Nonetheless, it also concerns membership of an organization, group or a community that involves a sense of solidarity (institutional/organizational level). These two parts are intrinsically linked: to be a member means to be actively engaged and to be actively engaged one has to be a member. One can be engaged in a specific activity only if one is a member and this is the reason why membership is seen as a pre-condition to participation. These aspects are not fully taken into consideration, and certainly not in the implementation of the Partecipa.Net projects. There is the impression that the main issue is to design devices which are able to support participation and that citizens will naturally take advantage of them. Nevertheless, this is not always the case as the participation rates of 'gli orari della città' and 'forum agorà' effectively demonstrates.

Political parties and trade unions are typical examples of organizations where participation takes place in the political arena. However, the presence of these organizations is not always equally represented across a region.[33] This requires seeing citizens as potential actors not only within organizations like political parties or trade unions but also in cultural, voluntary, trade associations, sports clubs, charities and parishes, etc. In this way, the focus shifts away from citizens and moves towards organizations and institutions which gives rise to the so-called civil society.

---

[32] Sidney Verba, Kay Lehman Schlozman and Henry Brady, *Voice and Equality: Civic Voluntarism in American Politics*, Harvard University Press, Cambridge, MA, 1995; Jon Elster, 'The market and the forum: three varieties of political theory', in Robert E. Goodin and Philip Pettit (eds), *Contemporary Political Philosophy: An Anthology*, Wiley Blackwell, Oxford, 1997.

[33] Angelo Panebianco, *Political Parties: Organisation and Power*, Cambridge University Press, Cambridge, 1988.

In this respect, organizations, institutions but also individual citizens can act as social brokers[34] as they are skilled and have expertise in networking. They bridge the gaps in relationships between people, groups, structures and even cultures facilitating the exchange of information and services between them. Social brokers are points of reference for specific networks due to factors such as expertise, knowledge and the charisma of the social broker, however, luck also plays an important role. For example, social brokers place themselves in places where people stop, talk, meet frequently and pass on information. In this respect, café-owners are a good example.

Can the local council, analysed above, be considered a social broker? Which other players can play a similar role without biasing the level of participation? Can municipalities stimulate the social, political and institutional context in order to bring together the number of players necessary to make participation effective and fruitful even through electronic means? The mapping of different forms through which the community activities take place, together with identifying the modes which citizens use to meet and interact with each other represents an alternative way to promote participation and also e-participation. These modes are places that constitute a point of reference for citizens and are considered appropriate spaces for expressing their social needs, for example.

The example of telecentres can be seen from this perspective. Telecentres can be subdivided into community telecentres, cyber cafés or Internet cafés and other connectivity services. Even though all of them provide public access to digital technologies, community telecentres characterize themselves because of the emphasis on social use. That is to say, the appropriation of the ITC tools and the information that can be accessed through them from a social change perspective enables innovative solutions to emerge. Social encounters, interaction, learning, personal growth and the mobilization of efforts to address community needs and problems are supported by this kind of public access. Cyber cafés tend to be for-profit businesses, providing basic e-mail, web browsing, electronic games and digital printing services, whereas the impact on social development is of a secondary importance. Of course, the attention is not focused on the connectivity and access services to the Internet provided by telecentres, but is directed towards developing places for improving social and political participation. These spaces are envisaged to be the nodes in which community information and information related to social services provided by local organizations can be made available. Nodes in which there is the possibility to attract voluntary work, to organize tutorial programmes on centres' operations, to develop advisory groups for supporting users and to establish links to other community organizations.

If all of the above is taken into consideration, the local council can easily be transformed into a telecentre or, at the very least, to promote the use of tools such as Partecipa.Net. It provides an environment in which participation is the common denominator and e-participation tools can render it more effective. The proliferation of e-participation tools in organizations such as local councils, cultural associations and the like can outline a new scenario in the level of participation: the traditional channels used to present social needs in the political arena are now integrated by new ones with a myriad of opportunities for actors to interact.

---

[34] Jeremy Boissevain, *Friends of Friends: Networks, Manipulators and Coalitions*, Basil Blackwell, Oxford, 1974.

Conclusions

This paper has analysed the development of the Participa.Net e-participation system, from its initial conceptual and planning phases through to its eventual implementation, in the region of Emilia Romagna. Consequently, it has been necessary to employ a dual perspective based on the concept of assemblage[35] in order to investigate Partecipa.Net enhancement, and in Heidegger's work on the phenomenology of religious life[36] in order to investigate its use in two specific contexts. Analysing this dual perspective has also provided an opportunity to focus on ontology issues. In particular, the sense of 'content', sense of 'relation' and sense of 'actualization' have been introduced as existential terms in the analysis of the phenomenon.

The consequences of introducing the stream of life in the analysis of social phenomena according to the perspective proposed, leads to a reconsideration of the role of theory in social research. Here, sense-making is not intended as a chain of events or as an established and rigorous order of entities. On the contrary, this rationale is exclusively connected to specific historical conditions rather than to a predefined order. It is from this understanding that the introduction of Partecipa.Net has been examined.

The objective has been to converge the sense of 'content', sense of 'relation' and sense of 'actualization' in order to move from an object-historical understanding to an enactment-historical one. In other words, the purpose has not been to generalize the specific results obtained following a specific theoretical approach, rather it is to gain an active scenario of e-participation tools in action.

From this perspective, some further considerations on the development of these projects are necessary. Unquestionably, a fruitful level of discussion had been reached which took shape in an environment that was supportive of the interactions which led to significant results. However, would it have been possible to arrive at similar decisions if a far larger number of participants would have joined the debate? Of course, a low participation rate creates the problem of representativeness. On the other hand, is it conceivable that thousands upon thousands of citizens actively join such electronic forms of participation?

In this respect, the case of the local council, mentioned in the above section, is particularly revealing. Its role is deemed to be a negative one due to the large presence of local councillors in the forum who biased the debate. However, the scenario could have been different if other councils would have joined the project. Why? Different and established positions would have an opportunity to challenge each other head-on. In some sense, a combination of representative democracy and deliberative democracy work together in harmony. A citizen would have the chance to promote his/her personal opinion on a specific issue and the same would be also true for pressure groups such as local councils. In this case, the exercising of participation rights would be articulated and lead to the development of an equilibrium between the possibility of voicing an opinion, on the one hand, and the representativeness of a specific position, on the other. Therefore, a rather ambivalent perspective can be used in order to achieve a higher level of democracy: a way of supporting the spread of e-participation tools

---

[35] Lanzara, op. cit.
[36] Heidegger, op. cit.

like Partecipa.Net to citizens and of mobilizing local councils to also adopt these instruments.

In the scenario outlined here, Municipalities are intended as the main protagonist of this policy. However, depending on the issue at stake, other local governments and institutions can also play a leading role in e-participation projects. Finally, the fact that Emilia Romagna is renowned on both a national and international level due to its large number of citizen associations[37] represents an exciting opportunity for engaging these institutions in social and political life, providing a fertile ground for introducing e-participation tools in everyday life.

Andrea Resca, after completing his PhD in 2009 at LUISS 'Guido Carli' University, Rome, Centre of Research on Information Systems (CeRSI) is continuing to do research at CeRSI. In 1999, he moved to South Korea where he obtained a Master of Arts in Korean Studies (International Area Studies). On returning to Italy in 2002, Andrea joined the 'Libera Università di Lingue e Comunicazione—IULM', Milan, as a Senior Research Fellow researching e-government, this research post lasted until 2005. His publications are diverse and range from organization theory to information systems, with e-government and e-participation being his current research domains.

---

[37] R. D. Putnam, R. Leonardi and R. Y. Nanetti, *Making Democracy Work: Civic Traditions in Modern Italy*, Princeton University Press, Princeton, NJ, 1994; D. Riley, 'Civic associations and authoritarian regimes in interwar Europe: Italy and Spain in comparative perspective', *American Sociological Review*, 70(2), 2005, pp. 288–310.

Learning from eParticipation initiatives of regional and local level authorities in Greece and Spain

ELENI PANOPOULOU, EFTHIMIOS TAMBOURIS, ELENA SANCHEZ-NIELSEN, MARIA ZOTOU and KONSTANTINOS TARABANIS

Introduction

Electronic Participation (eParticipation) is becoming a political priority for many European countries, often perceived as an essential ingredient of electronic government (eGovernment) policies. Strengthening of participation and democratic decision-making constitutes one of the five priorities adopted by the European Union (EU) in the i2010 e-Government Action Plan.[1] According to the EU *'e-government strategies at all levels should advance trust and confidence in public services and online democratic participation'*.[2] Also, in its recommendations on eDemocracy[3] the Council of Europe emphasizes the importance of maintaining and improving democratic institutions and processes in the context of the new opportunities and challenges arising from the information society. eParticipation emerges as a priority also at a global level. The United Nations suggest a three-step plan for enhancing eParticipation,[4,5] namely: (a) increasing e-information to citizens for decision-making; (b) enhancing e-consultation for deliberative and participatory processes; and (c) supporting e-decision-making by increasing the input of citizens in decision-making.

Intending to exploit this promising field, the EU has funded until 2008 more than 35 eParticipation research projects with a total budget of over €120 million mainly through the FP5 and the Preparatory Action programmes.[6] At the same time, a recent survey revealed what we perceive as a relatively small number of current eParticipation cases in Europe.[7,8] A result of that survey was that most

---

[1] European Commission, 'i2010 e-Government Action Plan: accelerating e-Government in Europe for the benefit of all', 173 final, 2006.

[2] European Commission, 'The role of e-Government for Europe's future', 567 final, 2003.

[3] Council of Europe, 'Recommendation of the Committee of Ministers to member states on electronic democracy', 2009.

[4] United Nations, 'e-Government readiness knowledge base', 2007.

[5] United Nations, 'eGovernment Survey 2008: from eGovernment to connected governance', 2008.

[6] Efthimios Tambouris, Evangelos Kalampokis and Konstantinos Tarabanis, 'A survey of e-participation research projects in the European Union', *International Journal of Electronic Business (IJEB)*, 6(6), 2008, pp. 554–571.

[7] Eleni Panopoulou, Efthimios Tambouris and Konstantinos Tarabanis, 'eParticipation initiatives: how is Europe progressing?', *European Journal of ePractice*, No. 7, March 2009.

[8] Eleni Panopoulou, Efthimios Tambouris and Konstantinos Tarabanis, 'D4.2c: eParticipation good practice cases and diffusion', *European eParticipation Study*, June 2009, available at: <http://islab.uom.gr/eP/>.

cases are to be found at the local and regional level than national, international and transnational.

Considering the above, eParticipation sounds like a flourishing field expected to grow even more in the following years. This makes it even more imperative to explore current initiatives in the field and try to learn from previous practice and experience. This paper focuses on learning from eParticipation initiatives offered by public authorities (PAs) at the regional and local levels of governance.

In the literature, frameworks for assessing eParticipation initiatives have only recently appeared.[9,10,11,12] These frameworks usually attempt a holistic evaluation of eParticipation, examining initiatives' different perspectives such as the processes followed, the outcomes achieved, the social and democratic value created, and various technical and project-related aspects. In this study, however, we mainly focus on eParticipation capabilities provided by websites of PAs. As a result, we concentrate on the relevant literature regarding website evaluation, where extensive references to suitable frameworks can be found.

It is well known from this literature that sophistication of websites is related to a number of characteristics, such as status visibility, user control and freedom, consistency and patterns, error prevention, aesthetics, etc.[13] Methods and tools have also been proposed to facilitate the process.[14,15] In the case of eGovernment, initial work has commenced on benchmarking,[16] however, at the same time, there is considerable discussion and criticism as to how eGovernment performance is measured.[17]

A few attempts have been made to propose and use specific metrics for assessing the websites of PAs. For example, it has been proposed that the websites of PAs should be assessed by considering accessibility, interoperability, security and privacy, information reliability, service agility and transparency. This approach has been used to evaluate 127 PA websites in Brazil.[18] It has been further proposed that criteria can be divided into two groups: information

---

[9] Ann Macintosh and Angus Whyte, 'Towards an evaluation framework for eParticipation', *Transforming Government: People, Process & Policy*, 2(1), 2008, pp. 16–30.

[10] Eleni Panopoulou, Efthimios Tambouris and Konstantinos Tarabanis, 'D4.1b: framework for eParticipation good practice', *European eParticipation Study*, November 2008, available at: <http://islab.uom.gr/eP/>.

[11] Georg Aichholzer and Hilmar Westholm, 'Evaluating eParticipation projects: practical examples and outline of an evaluation framework', *European Journal of ePractice*, No. 7, March 2009.

[12] Euripidis Loukis, Alexandros Xenakis and Yannis Charalabidis, 'An evaluation framework for e-participation in parliaments', *International Journal of Electronic Governance*, 3(1), 2010, pp. 25–47.

[13] Jakob Nielsen, *Designing WEB Usability: The Practice of Simplicity*, New Riders, Thousand Oaks, CA, 2000.

[14] Christian Bauer and Arno Scharl, 'Quantitative evaluation of Web site content and structure', *Internet Research: Electronic Networking Applications and Policy*, 10(1), 2000, pp. 31–43.

[15] Lili Wang, Stuart Bretschneider and Jon Gant, 'Evaluating Web-based e-government services with a citizen-centric approach', *Proceedings of the 38th Hawaii International Conference on System Sciences*, 2005.

[16] For example: European Commission, 'Benchmarking framework', i2010 High Level Group, 2006.

[17] Davy Janssen, 'Mine's bigger than yours: assessing international eGovernment benchmarking', in F. Bannister and D. Remenyi (eds), *3rd European Conference on eGovernment*, MCIL, Reading, 2003, pp. 209–218.

[18] Ana Christina Bicharra Garcia, Christiano Maciel and Fernando Bicharra Pinto, 'A quality inspection method to evaluate e-government sites', in Maria A. Wimmer *et al.* (eds), *EGOV 2005*, LNCS 3591, 2005, pp. 198–209.

content criteria (namely, orientation to website, content, currency, metadata, services, accuracy, privacy and external recognition) and ease of use criteria (namely, links, feedback mechanisms, accessibility, design and navigability). This approach was used to evaluate five websites of New Zealand government entities.[19] Furthermore, an E-Governance Performance Index, containing 98 measures, was used to evaluate municipal websites around the world.[20] However, citizens' online participation is the less evaluated concept of government websites; only two methods include such measures for assessing availability of bulletin boards, online surveys and polls[21,22] and utilization of chats, discussion forums, e-meetings and online decision-making mechanisms.[23]

All aforementioned approaches focus on measuring the supply side of PA websites. Although it has been suggested that the demand side should be equally evaluated,[24] in this paper we restrict our focus to measuring online sophistication of websites by employing measures that are independent of client involvement hence do not utilize metrics such as citizens' take-up, improvement of PAs' efficiency, etc.

The main objective of this paper is twofold. First, we evaluate eParticipation online sophistication of regional authorities' websites in Greece and Spain to determine how eParticipation is progressing at the regional level. For this purpose, we endorse a published evaluation framework for measuring online sophistication of PAs' websites. Second, we analyse one good practice case at the local level in each of the two countries and attempt to derive similarities and differences in eParticipation initiatives' implementation. Our analysis draws conclusions on the potential of regional and local level eParticipation, on issues to take into consideration when designing eParticipation initiatives and on lessons learnt.

The rest of this paper is organized as follows. In the next section we present the methodology followed in this work, including a short description of the evaluation framework used and of the gathered feedback on the local cases as well as the limitations of this work. The third section provides detailed information on the two countries under examination. Specifically it addresses the countries' administrative division, the electoral system for the regional and local levels and the policies in force relevant to the scope of this paper; eGovernment with a focus on eParticipation, and information and communication technology (ICT). Then, in the fourth section the results for both countries are presented, firstly at regional level and then at local level. Finally, a discussion of the results between the two countries is made in the fifth section. The paper concludes in the sixth section with a summary of our work and directions for future work.

---

[19] Alastair G. Smith, 'Applying evaluation criteria to New Zealand government websites', *International Journal of Information Management*, 21, 2001, pp. 137–149.

[20] Marc Holzer and Seang-Tae Kim, 'Digital governance in municipalities worldwide (2005): a longitudinal assessment of municipal websites throughout the world', *The E-Governance Institute*, 2005.

[21] Ibid.

[22] Anders T. Henriksson, Yiori Yi, Belinda Frost and Michael R. Middleton, 'Evaluation instrument for e-government web sites', *Proceedings Internet Research 7.0: Internet Convergences*, Brisbane, 2006.

[23] Holzer and Kim, op. cit.

[24] Janssen, op. cit.

E-PARTICIPATION IN SOUTHERN EUROPE AND THE BALKANS

Methodology

In this section we elaborate on the methodology followed in our survey. First, we introduce the evaluation framework used for measuring the sophistication of the regional authorities' websites and then we explain the sources of the local good practice cases and the limitations to our work.

Evaluation Framework for Regional Level Cases

For evaluating the eParticipation sophistication of websites of regional PAs we have applied the framework proposed by Panopoulou et al.,[25] and specifically the eParticipation axis of the framework. The eParticipation axis is structured based on the OECD levels of participation and includes three factors, namely, *information, consultation* and *active participation*[26] (Table 1). According to OECD, Information is a one-way channel that informs citizens about a variety of available resources; Consultation is a limited two-way channel; while Active Participation is a more enhanced two-way channel where citizens have more power over policy formulation.

For assessing the framework factors we employ overall six different metrics. For the information factor we employ a metric measuring the availability of online policy documents and the policy level these documents refer to. We differentiate between basic documents (minutes and decisions of council meetings), medium-level documents (basic documents plus council announcements) and high-level documents (medium-level documents plus different studies, e.g., financial and land-planning studies). For assessing the consultation factor we employ a metric measuring the availability of electronic consultations on the website. Finally, plese take in p 80 - a fram file for assessing the active participation factor we employ four different metrics. These refer to the availability of communication tools (chats, blogs and/or e-forums) and decision-making tools (e-polls), and to the ability for citizens to propose a topic at e-forums and e-polls as well as for inclusion in the agenda of the local representatives' meeting. It is worth noting here the difference between the e-consultations metric and the e-forums metric; e-consultations refer to the organized intention of the PA to get citizens' feedback on specific issues employing different ICT tools and techniques (even e-forums), while e-forums are regarded as a looser type of interaction, where both authority personnel and citizens may initiate different topics of interest and interact with each other.

The exact questionnaire used is provided in Table 2. Most of the questionnaire items are dichotomous and two items utilize nominal scales (one of them, metric 3, allowing multiple selection).

With regard to items scoring we award between 0 and 10 points for each question. Thus, dichotomous items are awarded with 0 or 10 points, and items measured in nominal scales may be awarded with different values between 0 and 10 depending on the answer. For developing an overall score for each website a

---

[25] Eleni Panopoulou, Efthimios Tambouris and Konstantinos Tarabanis, 'A framework for evaluating web sites of public authorities', *Aslib Proceedings: New Information Perspectives*, 60(5), 2008, pp. 517–546.

[26] OECD, *Citizens as Partners: OECD Handbook on Information, Consultation, and Public Participation in Policy-Making*, 2001.

Table 1. Factors, metrics and weights for evaluating eParticipation

Factors	Metrics evaluating	Factor weight
Information	Online policy documents	30%
Consultation	Electronic consultations	30%
Active Participation	Communication and decision-making tools, issues proposed by citizens	40%

Table 2. Questionnaire used and weighting of questions

Metric number	Question and possible answers	Metric weight
	Information factor	
Metric 1	Are policy documents available online? *No/Yes, basic documents/Yes, medium-level documents/Yes, high-level documents*	100%
	Consultation factor	
Metric 2	Are consultations on important local issues organized online (e-consultations)? *No/Yes*	100%
	Active Participation factor	
Metric 3	Is it possible for citizens to communicate through: *Chats/Blogs/eForums*	25%
Metric 4	Are polls organized online that refer to issues of local/regional interest and that are also incorporated into the decision process? *No/Yes*	25%
Metric 5	In the case that a discussion forum is available, is it possible for a citizen to initiate a new discussion topic? *No/Yes*	25%
Metric 6	Is it possible for citizens to provide a new agenda topic for discussion on the PA council meeting? *No/Yes*	25%

weighting scheme for factors and metrics is employed. For Information and Consultation factors we use a 100 per cent weight as each of them consists of only one metric. For the Active Participation factor we use 25 per cent weight for each of the four metrics so that each metric contributes equally to the factor's result. However, each factor does not contribute equally to the overall result; Information and Consultation contribute 30 per cent each, while Active Participation contributes 40 per cent. This is a decision made by the authors in order to reflect the notion that active participation is the third and most advanced level of participation.[27] The weighting scheme is also displayed in the last columns of Tables 1 and 2.

---

[27] Ibid.

The actual evaluation took place in two stages. Firstly, the evaluation of the websites of the Greek Regions and Prefectures was made in September–October 2008. Secondly, the evaluation of the websites of the Spanish Regions and Provinces took place in December 2008–January 2009. A different yet experienced evaluator has been involved in each evaluation stage. Finally, it should be noted that the websites were evaluated in the countries' official languages, Greek and Spanish.

Feedback on Local Level Cases

It would not be practical to perform a survey similar to the previous one at the local level due to the high number of local level administrations in both countries. Alternatively, we decided to focus on highlights of the local level by presenting and discussing one good practice case from each of the two countries. Both these cases can be considered as good practice due to the results they have already achieved and the distinctions they have gained.

Limitations

It should be acknowledged that the evaluation presented in this paper addresses only the supply side of eParticipation. For a more holistic evaluation one should also include a measurement of the demand side, namely, the actual participation and engagement of citizens through the presented eParticipation initiatives. This constitutes one of the next tasks which the authors consider undertaking.

A second limitation refers to the evaluation method employed for the regional authorities' websites. More specifically, all regional websites in this survey have been visited and evaluated from the perspective of the guest user. This means that the evaluators did not register on any of these websites for checking their full functionality for registered users. This decision was made in order to ensure fair consideration of all websites. For example, some websites in Spain contain a private area for registered users which offers discussion possibilities with representatives of the authorities. However, the credentials for accessing this private area are provided by the city councils to inhabitants. This suggests that it was not possible for the evaluators to access this area; nevertheless, there was available information to the guest user on the discussion capabilities within the private area so these websites were considered in the results.

A third limitation refers to the fact that it has not been possible for the authors to perform a thorough survey at the local level due to time and effort restrictions inherent in such a wide survey. However, the selected cases have been cited in other larger scale surveys and award schemes; it is therefore anticipated that they are indeed good practice cases worthy of being noted here for drawing our conclusions.

The Two Countries

Spain and Greece display a similar population density, around 86 inhabitants per km^2,[28] and they are both Mediterranean countries implying some similarities

---

[28] Eurostat, 'Population density', <http://epp.eurostat.ec.europa.eu/portal/page?_pageid = 1996,39140985&_dad = portal&_schema = PORTAL&screen = detailref&language = en&pro

in mentality and culture. However, in Information Society indicators Greece lags well behind Spain; households with Internet connection in Greece are 31 per cent as opposed to 51 per cent in Spain, and considering broadband Internet this percentage drops to 22 and 45 per cent, respectively. Regarding Internet usage for interacting with PAs in Greece only 8.8 per cent have obtained information online, 4 per cent have downloaded forms and 3.6 per cent have returned completed forms using the Internet. For Spain the same indicators rise to 28.6, 15.7 and 8.5 per cent, respectively.[29]

Greece

At the time the survey was conducted, regional level Greece comprised two tiers of administration; Peripheries (Regions) and Prefectures. Specifically, the official regional administrative divisions of Greece were the 13 Regions[30] and the 57 Prefectures.[31] General Secretaries of Regions were not directly elected by the people but appointed by the Greek government; however, prefectural councils and prefects were (since 1994) elected by the people every four years.

Nevertheless, the newly appointed government from the October 2009 national elections has in the meantime performed a radical reform of regional and local public administration. According to the 'Kallikratis' plan that was fully implemented in 2010, Greece now comprises only two tiers of regional and local administration; Regions remain 13, Prefectures no longer exist and Municipalities have been merged into approximately one-third of their previous number of 1034. Moreover, citizens now elect the representatives for both tiers of administration, Regions and Municipalities.

The priorities regarding ICT development in Greece have been set out in the 'Digital Strategy 2006–2013' document,[32] and although different aspects of eGovernment are included, such as e-procurement and provision of electronic services to citizens, it does not include any reference to eParticipation or eDemocracy. Notably enough, an older governmental white paper on the development of the Information Society in Greece,[33] refers to strengthening of the democratic processes through ICT and includes *'encouraging greater participation of citizens in matters of common interest'* as one of its goals. Specifically, in this paper each regional authority is invited to prepare its own plan for the Information Society aimed among others at *'increasing public awareness and active participation in public matters'*. Moreover, the Operational Programme for the Information Society (OPIS),[34] an innovative horizontal programme cutting across government departments and aiming at implementing the essential features of the Greek Government's Information Society White Paper sets as an objective to strengthen civic democratic participation and transparency.

Footnote 28 continued
duct = EU_MAIN_TREE&root = EU_MAIN_TREE/tb/t_popul/t_popula/t_pop/t_demo_gen/tps00003>.

[29] All percentages sourced from Eurostat and are provided in the official national factsheets in ePractice.eu: <http://www.epractice.eu/en/factsheets/>.

[30] According to the official Greek Regions' website: <http://www.perifereies.gov.gr/>.

[31] According to the Union of Prefectural Authorities in Greece: <http://www.enae.gr/>.

[32] Ministry of Economy and Finance, Digital Strategy 2006–2013, 2005.

[33] Greece in the Information Society, Strategy and Actions, 2002.

[34] <http://www.infosoc.gr/infosoc/en-UK/epktp/default.htm>.

Spain

Spain is divided into 17 Regions, called Autonomous Communities, with regional governments that were created following the guidelines established in the democratic Constitution ratified in 1978.[35] The second article of the Constitution recognizes the rights of Autonomous Communities to self-government. There are 50 Provinces in Spain that are formed by groups of municipalities each with their own council. Each of the 17 Regions[36] consists of one or more of the 50 Provinces. Municipal Councils are directly elected by the electors. Provincial representatives in Spain are elected by the citizens every four years as in Greece; however, each Autonomous Community in Spain due to the power of self-government has its own president, government and Supreme Court[37] holding thus more power than the corresponding regional authorities in Greece.

The priorities set out for the development of the Information Society in Spain[38,39] and for the modernization of the Spanish Administration[40] focus more on issues such as provision of qualitative services to citizens, new digital infrastructures and improvement of public administration processes than on promoting eParticipation. However, modernization also provides for measures aiming among others to the establishment of an online area dedicated to public eConsulting on normative projects or government decisions. Additionally, eParticipation concerns are also mentioned as challenges to be faced by the Spanish public administration.[41]

Results

In this section we provide the findings of our work; the first subsection presents the evaluation results of regional authorities' websites in Greece and Spain, and the second subsection provides a long description of two good practice cases at the local level in the two countries under examination.

Regional Level

Greece. Overall, the websites of 12 Regions and 46 Prefectures have been evaluated in Greece and the results are presented below. The remaining websites (1 Region and 11 Prefectures) are not included in the reported results because they were either under construction or not in operation during the evaluation period.

---

[35] Kingdom of Spain, Public Administration Country Profile, Division for Public Administration and Development Management, Department of Economic and Social Affairs, United Nations, April 2006.

[36] Wikipedia, 'Autonomous communities of Spain', <http://en.wikipedia.org/wiki/Autonomous_communities_of_Spain>.

[37] Ministerio de Administraciones Públicas, Constitución, <http://www.map.es/documentacion/legislacion/constitucion.html>.

[38] Ministerio de Industria, Turismo y Comercio, Plan Avanza 2006–2010, 2005.

[39] Ministerio de Industria, Turismo y Comercio, Plan Avanza2 2009–2012, 2009.

[40] Ministerio de Administraciones Públicas, Plan Moderniza 2006–2008.

[41] Ministry of Public Administration, 'White paper on the improvement of public services', 2nd ed., 2000.

Table 3. Overall results for regional authorities' websites in Greece

Overall results	Regions	Prefectures	Total
Information	0.00%	16.85%	13.36%
Consultation	25.00%	17.39%	18.97%
Active Participation	0.00%	8.26%	6.55%
Weighted average	7.50%	13.58%	12.32%

Table 4. Detailed results for regional authorities' websites in Greece

Metric number	Questions and answers			
	Information factor			
Metric 1	Are policy documents available online?			
	No	Yes, basic documents	Yes, medium-level documents	Yes, high-level documents
Regions	100%	0%	0%	0%
Prefectures	67.4%	30.43%	2.17%	0%
Total	74.14%	24.14%	1.72%	0%
	Consultation factor			
Metric 2	Are consultations on important local issues organized online (e-consultations)?			
	No	Yes		
Regions	75%	25%		
Prefectures	82.6%	17.4%		
Total	81.03%	18.97%		
	Active Participation factor			
Metric 3	Is it possible for citizens to communicate through:			
	Chats	Blogs	eForums	
Regions	0%	0%	0%	
Prefectures	0%	0%	6.52%	
Total	0%	0%	5.17%	
Metric 4	Are polls organized online that refer to issues of local/regional interest and that are also incorporated into the decision process?			
	No	Yes		
Regions	100%	0%		
Prefectures	71.74%	28.26%		
Total	77.59%	22.41%		
Metric 5	In the case that a discussion forum is available, is it possible for a citizen to initiate a new discussion topic?			
	No	Yes		
Regions	–	–		
Prefectures	66.67%	33.33%		
Total	66.67%	33.33%		
Metric 6	Is it possible for citizens to provide a new agenda topic for discussion on the PA council meeting?			
	No	Yes		
Regions	100%	0%		
Prefectures	100%	0%		
Total	100%	0%		

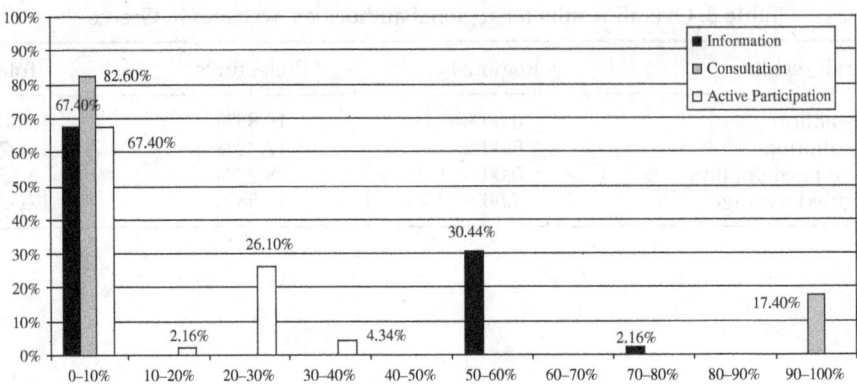

Figure 1. Score frequencies for Prefectures in Greece.

The overall results for regional authorities' websites in Greece are provided in Table 3, while in Table 4 the detailed results for each metric are provided.

Greek Regions do not offer policy documents online or any features that promote the active participation of citizens, scoring an absolute zero at these metrics. The reason might be that Regions in Greece do not yet have any significant legislative power. Indeed, the General Secretary of Regions is not directly elected but rather is appointed by the government. With regards to e-consultation, only one-fourth of Regions offer relevant online facilities, indicating their intention to engage citizens in discussion on regional matters.

On the other hand, Greek Prefectures offer some information, consultation and active participation possibilities to citizens. Around 30 per cent of Prefectures offer basic policy documents online and even less (approximately 17 per cent) organize online consultations. Greek Prefectures' websites offer no chat or blog facilities although a limited number of them (6.52 per cent) offer online discussion forums in which it is usually possible for citizens to initiate discussions. Only approximately 28 per cent conduct polls online and no Greek Prefecture offers the possibility to citizens to propose agenda topics for the council meetings. Obviously, Greek Prefectures utilize different eParticipation opportunities at different degrees. As presented in Figure 1, most Prefectures gathered low scoring in all participation levels. Nevertheless, around 30 per cent of them seem to offer adequate information and active consultation opportunities, while 15 per cent offer e-consultation features.

Spain. Overall, the websites of 17 Regions and 40 Provinces have been evaluated in Spain and the results are presented below. It should be noted that the five Regions that include only one Province and consequently offer one website for both the Region and the Province authorities have been calculated within the Regions' figures. The remaining websites (5 Provinces) are not included in the reported results because they were either not in operation or non-existent during the evaluation period. The overall results for regional authorities' websites in Spain are provided in Table 5, while in Table 6 the detailed results for each metric are provided.

Table 5. Overall results for regional authorities' websites in Spain

Overall results	Regions	Provinces	Total
Information	73.53%	73.13%	73.25%
Consultation	17.65%	17.50%	17.54%
Active participation	1.76%	1.38%	1.49%
Weighted average	28.06%	27.74%	27.83%

Contrary to Greece, most of Spain's regional authorities have adopted a specific template for offering and organizing content on their websites. This is the reason for the high similarity between the scores of Regions and Provinces in Tables 5 and 6.

At the information level nearly all websites in Spain gathered a very good score, as they provide online medium-level policy documents for citizens (Table 6). At the consultation level only 17.5 per cent of the Regions' and Provinces' websites provide e-consultation facilities, and finally at the active participation level nearly all websites score close to 1 per cent, with some exceptions; around 3 per cent of Provinces offer online chats, e-polls and discussion forums while 8 per cent of them offer online blogs, and around 11 per cent of Regions offer online blogs and forums. However, none of the Regions and Provinces that offer online discussion forums provide the possibility to citizens to initiate new discussion topics and none of the Spanish regional websites offer the possibility to citizens to propose a new agenda topic for the local council. Due to the aforementioned similarity of findings for Regions and Provinces, we provide the score frequencies for all websites in Spain in one figure (Figure 2). The figure clearly shows that most Spanish regional websites score very poorly in consultation and active participation factors, while most of them score really well at the information factor.

Comparison of results at regional level. A comparison of the overall results for Greece and Spain is provided in Table 7. At the information level, Spain has a very big advantage over Greece scoring in average around 60 per cent more. On the contrary, at the active participation level and although both countries display low scores, Greece has a clear advantage over Spain. Nonetheless, both countries' regional authorities seem to place a similar emphasis on e-consultation facilities, scoring both around 17 per cent.

When comparing the results per Regions or Prefectures/Provinces in the two countries, the conclusions are fairly the same (Figure 3). There is only one additional observation to be made, that at the active participation level only Greek Prefectures score better than Spanish Regions and Provinces; as explained previously Greek Regions scored 0 per cent at information provision and active participation.

Additionally, it is worth noting that overall Greek Regions are performing worse than all other regional authorities in the two countries. As mentioned previously, the reason for this may be that responsibilities of Greek Regions are relatively limited; they do not have legislative power and are not elected directly by the citizens. However, it would be interesting to examine if this will change in the next years after the administrative reform in Greece has been completed and

Table 6. Detailed results for regional authorities' websites in Spain

Metric number	Questions and answers			
Metric 1	*Information factor* Are policy documents available online?			
	No	Yes, basic documents	Yes, medium-level documents	Yes, high-level documents
Regions	0%	5.88%	94.12%	0%
Provinces	2.50%	0%	97.50%	0%
Total	1.755%	1.755%	96.49%	0%
Metric 2	*Consultation factor* Are consultations on important local issues organized online (e-consultations)?			
	No	Yes		
Regions	82.35%	17.65%		
Provinces	82.50%	17.50%		
Total	82.46%	17.54%		
Metric 3	*Active Participation factor* Is it possible for citizens to communicate through:			
	Chats	Blogs	eForums	
Regions	0%	11.76%	11.76%	
Provinces	3%	8%	3%	
Total	1.75%	8.77%	5.26%	
Metric 4	Are polls organized online that refer to issues of local/regional interest and that are also incorporated into the decision process?			
	No	Yes		
Regions	100%	0%		
Provinces	97.50%	2.5%		
Total	98.24%	1.76%		
Metric 5	In the case that a discussion forum is available, is it possible for a citizen to initiate a new discussion topic?			
	No	Yes		
Regions	100%	0%		
Provinces	100%	0%		
Total	100%	0%		
Metric 6	Is it possible for citizens to provide a new agenda topic for discussion on the PA council meeting?			
	No	Yes		
Regions	100%	0%		
Provinces	100%	0%		
Total	100%	0%		

Regions hold enhanced political power. On the contrary, Spanish Regions are already much more autonomous with self-government, where the Spanish Constitution provides the separation between legislative, executive and judiciary power. However, this autonomy makes even more interesting the finding that websites of Spanish regional authorities follow a similar template, while in Greece that no such autonomy is observed a similar approach has not been adopted.

Although Greece and Spain have improved their eGovernment readiness since 2005, it could be concluded from this survey that neither country's regional

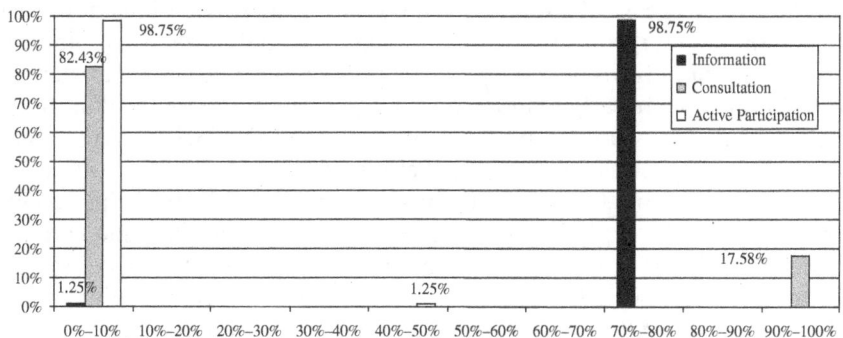

Figure 2. Score frequencies for Regions and Provinces in Spain.

Table 7. Overall results for regional authorities' websites in Greece and Spain

Overall results	Greece	Spain
Information	13.36%	73.25%
Consultation	18.97%	17.54%
Active Participation	6.55%	1.49%
Total	12.32%	27.83%

authorities are adequately advanced in eParticipation. Of course, Spain performs very well as far as information provision, namely, availability of policy documents, is concerned. However, when it comes to more engaging participatory features such as e-consultations, e-forums, e-polls, etc. only a few regional

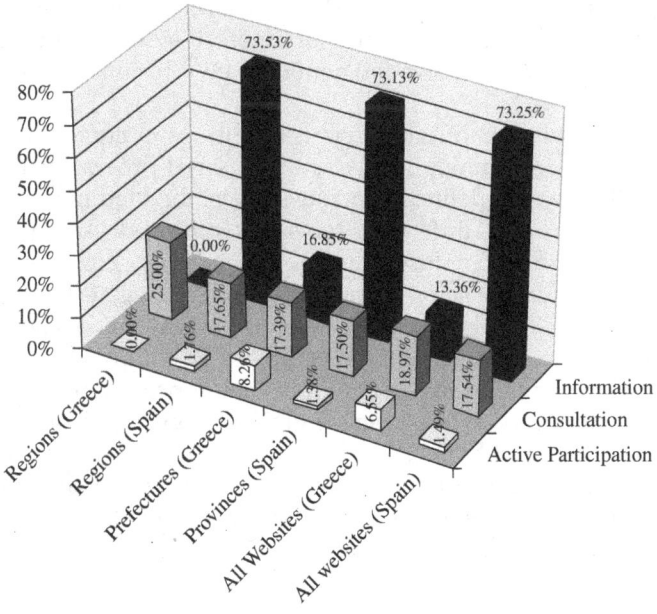

Figure 3. Comparison of Greek and Spanish Regions and Prefectures/Provinces.

authorities in Greece and Spain offer such opportunities. Especially at the active participation level results are discouraging; not only are there not many opportunities for citizens to actively participate but also nearly no evidence has been found that such participation could be 'heard' by the regional authorities. These poor results could be partially attributed to the lack of governmental strategic planning for adopting such eParticipation opportunities although the EU's strategic plan for eGovernment aims to increase public participation in the political process. As explained previously, both countries' strategic and policy documents on the Information Society do not include specific goals or measures for eParticipation especially when it comes to its adoption at the regional or local level. Parallel to this situation, an increasing number of citizens are creating their personal eParticipation initiatives by means of their own blogs and posting individual views and ideas.

Local Level

For investigating eParticipation initiatives at the local level in the two countries we present two good practice cases.

E-dialogue in the city of Trikala, Greece. The objective of e-dialogos,[42,43] a European eGovernment awards 2009 finalist, is to offer all citizens the opportunity to get involved directly in the process of development and implementation of city policies through an online platform of dialogue and participation, in an effort to reverse the disengagement of citizens with their elected representatives and the policy process.

Since May 2007 when it was first launched, the platform comprises three e-tools: (i) a top-down e-Survey system, where the municipality can ask citizens to respond to specific issues of interest to the municipality; (ii) a bottom-up e-Petition system; and (iii) a moderated e-forum with a fully fledged e-deliberation process.

The major innovation of the project lies in its unique methodology of deliberation. The e-deliberation is essentially a 'serial process' within a specific timeframe, with five well-defined concrete steps embedded in each deliberative cycle. Within this process, different e-tools are employed. An e-poll serves the agenda setting stage, the e-forum is moderated and hosts pre-determined threads, and an e-survey helps to quantify and aggregate the results of the e-forum. Finally, there is also an interactive online real-time webcast of the city council proceedings where citizens can offer their feedback directly. The developed information platform, supports the provision of information at every stage of the process, even per single question posed or per discussion thread (the so-called 'fact bank').

Considering the issues e-dialogos faced until securing a smooth implementation and operation and the valuable experience gained, there are numerous lessons to be learnt for similar initiatives:

---

[42] e-dialogos project, <http://www.edialogos.gr>.
[43] <http://www.epractice.eu/en/cases/edialogosawards>.

(1) Convincing key people (funders, elected representatives, city council, administrative staff, etc.) about the scope and benefits of the project is an important success factor. The champions in the case of e-dialogos have been the Mayor and the CEO of the coordinating body (e-trikala).
(2) Recognizing that there are no ready-made transferable solutions or one-size fits all platform or methodology, and that tailor-made solutions still need the input of a wide range of experts (software developers, social scientists, opinion poll experts, communication experts, content managers, graphic designers, etc.) to collaborate as one team that will take into account the local needs and restrictions (cultural, political, technical).
(3) Careful budget planning so that all necessary components (i.e. moderators' training, advertising, content development, etc.) are properly budgeted from the start.
(4) Putting emphasis on interface design in order to make it user-friendly and as accessible and inclusive as possible. At the same time the platform should be kept scalable and replicable for other occasions and partners.
(5) Establishing an effective and sustainable management with one dedicated senior person being responsible for the project's operation. Moreover, adequate training of moderators and operators of the project is critical.
(6) Developing a solid communications strategy to 'educate' the owners, the users, the management team and remaining stakeholders of the project employing both online and offline methods. In specific, e-dialogos developed a communication plan which ensured that citizens had the means to get informed about the project, that the information offered was balanced, non-partisan and easy to access, and most importantly that created a level of trust and expectation to the stakeholders. All this, combined with the strong commitment of the city and its mayor and the dominant position that the city holds with respect to ICT adoption, have created a 'culture of participation' which is the single most important outcome from the project.

Madrid Participa by city of Madrid, Spain. The Madrid Participa project,[44] a European eGovernment awards 2007 finalist, is an instrument based on an e-consultation platform to increase citizen participation in the decision-making process in the city of Madrid. Since 2004 the City Council of Madrid has gained valuable experience and lessons learnt by running more than 20 e-consultations in various city districts.

Participa is a project aiming at the following: (i) to foster citizen engagement in local governance by means of participation through new technologies and to overcome the reticence and difficulties of the population; (ii) to provide citizens with electronic means to participate in the local decision-making processes that directly affect them, especially by the use of e-consultations; (iii) to increase awareness of the numerous public access Internet centres deployed throughout the city since 2004; and (iv) to check that the technologies used meet the necessary security and stringency requirements to guarantee democratic decision-making. As a result, the project Madrid Participa has influenced the way the decisions are made in the Council units using the e-consultation platform, as now they can

---

[44] Madrid Participa project, <http://www.madridparticipa.org>.

consider citizens' opinion regarding key issues as another factor in the decision-making process.

The main innovation of Madrid Participa project is the use of a secure e-voting system with a multi-channel approach focused on the use of new technologies and the usage of traditional polling stations with paper ballots. The different approaches supported with the new technologies were remote electronic participation from a personal computer with an Internet connection, onsite electronic participation from computers provided in municipals' permanent public Internet centres and remote electronic participation from mobile telephones.

Again, there are many lessons to be gained by the Madrid Participa project[45] as follows:

(1) The necessity to offer voters multiple voting channels (new voting technologies and traditional voting mechanisms) to guarantee their participation.
(2) Ensuring that security issues and concerns in a multi-channel e-voting system are dealt with adequately in order to generate trust among stakeholders and mostly citizens.
(3) Paying attention to the platform interface related to citizen registration and voting processes; it should be simple in order to increase participation rates.
(4) Devising a good communications plan with intensive efforts to broadcast the initiative using neighbours' associations, and with the purpose of reaching more citizens with almost no extra cost and becoming more sensitive about their needs and preferences.

Discussion

Considering the aforementioned findings at regional and at local level and the experience from the work presented above we are able to draw some conclusions regarding the actual elements to be considered by the PAs that wish to implement eParticipation solutions. Our conclusions are summarized below.

Planning is a very important step. A well thought out methodology for laying out and maintaining the eParticipation initiative that considers the specificities of each area and audience is of outmost importance during the planning phase. For really engaging citizens, it is not enough for example to implement some scattered eParticipation tools according to a national or European strategy; similarly, it is not enough to select eParticipation tools simply because they have been used elsewhere with success. Planning should include considering the citizens' circumstances and needs (i.e. cultural characteristics, relationship with politics and governmental processes, educational level, technological knowledge, professional and social status, nationality, etc.) and interpreting them into a specific tools mix and into a specific integrated participation process that are the most suitable for the area at hand.

And even from the planning phase and throughout the implementation it is important to ensure the involvement and sponsoring of key, high-level persons

---

[45] Carlos González Esteban, Madrid Participa, ePractice.eu, 2010, <http://www.epractice.eu/en/cases/madridp>.

from the PA. The feeling from the survey presented in this paper and from other similar work we have performed in the past is that majority of initiatives are not adequately driven by higher management, and thus suffer the consequence of being gradually neglected and abandoned even though authorities may have invested considerable funds and effort into implementing them.

But even at the lower management level, daily support and maintenance at the technical, procedural and content level are essential. A dedicated person is needed to ensure the decided methodology is followed, to quickly provide feedback to participants and stimulate further participation (moderation), to summarize results and forward them to the appropriate decision-makers and to report back to the audience on how their feedback has been used and with what results.

The need for a simple, intuitive and user-friendly platform interface may sound as a common recommendation made for any ICT implementation. However, experience has shown that eParticipation systems need to ensure that users understand a platform's functionality within the first minutes of use. Considering also the importance inclusion plays in any eParticipation initiative, it is evident that a good user interface as well as multiple entry points and channels (home PCs, public kiosks, mobile phones, etc.) have the potential to leverage the quantity and quality of participation.

Possibly because PAs are used to being sought after by citizens in need of public services instead of seeking to 'sell' their services to citizens, they usually neglect the marketing and promotion of the eParticipation opportunities they offer. Both good practice cases we presented previously placed increased emphasis on a sound communication plan and this has been proven beneficial for their case. On the contrary, the fact that in some regional authorities' websites the eParticipation features are located deeply in the submenus is an indication that not adequate attention has been paid to promoting the initiative.

Finally, when it comes to voting or any other decision-making mechanisms, it is important to ensure absolute security and privacy for the participants. Utilizing reliable security mechanisms and communicating this to the public and the remaining stakeholders assists both in providing reliable results and in overcoming any initial concerns and citizens' reticence.

Returning to the two countries under examination, and although Greece and Spain have improved their eGovernment readiness since 2005, it could be concluded that neither country's PAs are adequately advanced in eParticipation. Our survey at the regional level showed relatively poor results; only information provision in Spain seems to be advanced at a satisfying level. Information provision in Greece as well as consultation opportunities in both countries are mediocre, while active participation is practically non-existent in both countries. Of course, there are some bright examples like the two local cases presented in this paper, however, overall it does not seem like PAs in Greece and Spain are making substantial efforts into integrating eParticipation in their usual business. During our survey on regional websites we have not been able to examine these initiatives in full detail; however, we found no evidence that there was an organized effort to integrate eParticipation with internal processes. Moreover, almost no evidence has been found that such eParticipation efforts could be 'heard' by the regional authorities as in most of the cases there was no feedback on how the contributions are used and with what outcomes.

These poor results could be partially attributed to the countries' economic, political, social/cultural and technological landscape. For example, the combination of negative gross domestic product (GDP) growth, rising unemployment and a high deficit has led to the lack of trust in the democratic process and the institutions managing the process. Moreover, in the context of social and cultural environment, education is a precondition to being able to utilize Internet services and solutions. Nevertheless, recent statistics show an increase in engagement among the youth population with various internet services, which is promising for better take-up of eParticipation initiatives in the future. Furthermore, the lack of national effort to support digital technology in schools in primary and secondary education in the past has also introduced a slowdown in the acquisition of technical skills in the educational levels to support currently the citizens' digital interaction. Like in other European countries from the technological point of view, the user interface, the lack of understanding as how to engage and focus are not 'attractive' enough to the stakeholders involved including politicians, municipal administration, citizens and interest groups. At the same time, the lack of governmental strategic planning for introducing and adopting eParticipation opportunities is also a key issue to face the challenge of increasing citizen engagement; although at the present time the EU's strategic plan for eGovernment aims to increase public participation in the political process. As explained previously, both countries' strategic and policy documents on the Information Society do not include specific goals or measures for eParticipation especially when it comes to its adoption at the regional or even local level. Parallel to this situation, an increasing number of citizens are creating their personal forms of eParticipation, e.g. through their own blogs and are posting their views for the world to see. Overall, it is evident that both countries have a long way to go in order to be able to fully exploit the advantages of eParticipation.

Conclusion

In this paper we investigate eParticipation progress of regional and local PAs in Greece and Spain. For this purpose we have conducted a twofold analysis. At the regional level we have evaluated the eParticipation online sophistication of regional authorities' websites employing a suitable published framework. At the local level, where a similar survey of thousands of PAs' websites is prohibitive in terms of cost and effort, we have analysed one good practice case per country. Based on these analyses we attempt to draw conclusions on how eParticipation initiatives of PAs are progressing in the two countries and what lessons can be learnt in the process.

We recognize there are inherit limitations in the work presented in this paper. Apart from the lack of a thorough survey at the local level which was previously explained, we should also mention that website evaluation at the regional level has been conducted only from the visitor's (not the registered user's) perspective due to difficulties of registering on some Spanish websites. Last but not least, we should also recognize that our survey examines only the supply side of eParticipation; obviously, it would be interesting to also measure the demand side for drawing comprehensive conclusions.

The authors consider different plans for future work. One idea is to expand the survey at the regional level in other European countries, although the main identified restriction is the language barrier. Another idea is to enhance the evaluation framework with input from the supply side, meaning the actual participants, for example, through considering the quantity and quality of participation in each case. However, many restrictions are to be identified in this, as for example the fact that many online voting tools require credentials which can only be provided to proven residents of the area.

Acknowledgements

Parts of the work presented in this paper were conducted within a national project and a European project undertaken by the University of Macedonia team. Specifically, the methodology for evaluating the PAs' websites has been developed under a project concerning ICT utilization in Greek regional and local governments, which was funded by the Observatory for the Greek Information Society, while information on the two cases presented has been borrowed from the European eParticipation study, a service contract funded by the European Commission. We should also note that this paper revisits and extends the results presented in the International Conference for eParticipation (ePart2009) in Linz, Austria.[46]

Eleni Panopoulou is a researcher at the University of Macedonia, Thessaloniki, Greece since 2006. She holds an Electrical and Computer Engineering degree from AUTH and an MBA from the University of Surrey. She is involved in different eGovernment research projects and studies, with a special focus on eGovernment services provision and eParticipation.

Efthimios Tambouris is an Assistant Professor at the University of Macedonia, Thessaloniki, Greece. He has served at research centres (CERTH, NCSR) and in industry. He has more than 80 scientific publications in eGovernment and eParticipation and is co-chair of the International Conference on eParticipation (ePart).

Elena Sanchez-Nielsen, doctorate in Computer Science and Artificial Intelligence, is director of research of different projects related to eGovernment and eParticipation. She is associate professor in the Department of Computer Science and Systems at the University of La Laguna, Spain. She has authored scientific papers in the field of Artificial Intelligence, Intelligent Systems and eGovernment.

---

[46] Eleni Panopoulou, Efthimios Tambouris, Maria Zotou and Konstantinos Tarabanis, 'Evaluating eParticipation sophistication of regional authorities websites: the case of Greece and Spain', in Ann Macintosh and Efthimios Tambouris (eds), *ePart 2009*, LNCS 5694, 2009, pp. 67–77.

Maria Zotou is a researcher at the University of Macedonia, Thessaloniki, Greece since 2007. She holds a diploma in Information Technology from the Department of Applied Informatics of the University of Macedonia and is now studying for her master's in the area of eLearning. E-mail: mzotou@uom.gr

Konstantinos Tarabanis is a Professor at the Department of Business Administration of the University of Macedonia, Thessaloniki, Greece. In his yearlong career he has authored several research publications in the areas of software modelling and information systems' development for eGovernment, eBusiness, eLearning and eManufacturing.

Using participative GIS and e-tools for involving citizens of Marmo Platano–Melandro area in European programming activities

BENIAMINO MURGANTE, LUCIA TILIO, VIVIANA LANZA and FRANCESCO SCORZA

Introduction

Traditional methods adopted in planning and programming activities have been developed in periods when society was less dynamic and complex. Such approaches led to defining the future evolution of a territory in great detail.[1] The application of these methods in the current context of socio-economic transformation coupled with abrupt changes due to technological innovation, globalization and recent financial crisis contributed to the creation of a sort of 'suspiciousness' about planning and programming activities. Plans following such assumptions based their success on a faithful execution of planning instruments,[2] but the extreme mutability of today's socio-economic contexts may lead to the risk of discussing once again the location choices made many years before.

In the present work, we use the 'programming' term to denote all government tools regulating the public economic investments for local development. In particular, we considered the hierarchy of intervention tools at different scales promoted by EU policies in different sectors: regional convergence, environment, education, social capital, etc. In our opinion, the programme is a particular part of planning activities connected more to economic resource management than to physical territorial dimensions. Programming activities influence territorial planning at different scales, but also implement several actions not directly connected to territorial transformations. For this reason, it is relevant to distinguish between the two terms.

Since the 1960s, different approaches to strategic planning have been theorized. The main difference can be found in a sort of transition from a purely top-down approach to a 'reticular interactive' one, where the knowledge and imagination of society play a fundamental role in order to discover desirable scenarios.[3] Such differences define three major families of strategic

---

[1] R. Camagni, 'La città come impresa, l'impresa come piano, il piano come rete: tre metafore per intendere il significato del piano in condizioni di incertezza', in F. Curti and M. C. Gibelli (eds), *Pianificazione strategica e gestione dello sviluppo urbano*, Alinea, Firenze, 1996, pp. 83–98.

[2] L. Mazza, 'Descrizione e Previsione', in S. Lombardo and G. Preto, *Innovazione e Trasformazioni della Città, Teorie Metodi e Programmi per il mutamento*, Franco Angeli, Milano, 1993.

[3] M. C. Gibelli, 'Riflessioni sulla pianificazione strategica', in R. Rosini (ed.), *L'urbanistica delle aree metropolitane*, Alinea, Firenze, 1992.

plans.[4] The first family, largely used during the 1960s and 1970s, was based on a top-down approach and essentially referred to the rational comprehensive approach to planning. In the 1980s, a short-term approach to strategic planning was adopted. It was based on corporate planning, implying a pragmatic behaviour which may lead to a strong territorial deregulation. In the 1990s, a reticular and visionary approach to strategic planning was used. According to Harvard[5] and Minnesota models,[6] SWOT analysis plays a central role in order to examine internal and external environments,[7] producing also a stakeholder analysis considering organizations, groups, persons and all citizens, who can have a key influence on strategic processes. Other important aspects of this family of strategic plans are:

- the development of a vision for the future;
- the identification of general goals and specific objectives;
- the definition of strategies (how they actually fulfil goals and objectives);
- the evaluation of the progress of the action implementation of strategies.

This family considers strategic planning as a form of governance implementation. This concept represents a new approach to public administration. There has been a transition from an approach based on direct action (Government), where the Local Authority contributes directly to problem solution, to another approach where the Local Authority tends to manage the process (Governance),[8] where the administration makes possible and facilitates a search for different solutions, in cooperation and agreement with other public and private subjects.[9] Obviously, in case of changing contexts, iterative processes are possible and flexibility is also crucial to avoid bureaucratization. The 'reticular' term means that the strategic plan cannot be implemented only by a single local authority, but by a group of different levels of public administrations (be they elected by citizens or not). This term means also that there is the widest possible involvement of all potential stakeholders in order to avoid possible conflicts which could stall the whole process and, above all, to create a broad and shared planning vision. Visioning concerns not only actors, who can be represented by institutions, but it also considers the possibility that collective knowledge and imagination may stimulate a search for optimal solutions. Such interactivity, aiming at a wide stakeholder involvement, is undoubtedly difficult to achieve using traditional participation. Nowadays, a lot of successful initiatives have been developed, adopting the 'share' term as an imperative. These positive experiences based on mass collaboration

---

[4] M. C. Gibelli, 'Tre famiglie di piani strategici: verso un modello "reticolare" e "visionario"', in M. C. Gibelli and F. Curti (eds), *Pianificazione strategica e gestione dello sviluppo urbano*, Alinea, Firenze, 1996.

[5] J. M. Bryson and R. C. Einsweiler, 'Strategic planning: introduction', *Journal of the American Planning Association*, 53(1), 1987, pp. 6–8.

[6] J. M. Bryson, *Strategic Planning for Public and Nonprofit Organizations: A Guide to Strengthening and Sustaining Organizational Achievement*, John Wiley, San Francisco, 2004.

[7] J. M. Bryson and R. C. Einsweiler (eds), *Strategic Planning: Threats and Opportunities for Planners*, Planners Press, American Planning Association, Chicago, IL and Washington, DC, 1988.

[8] A. Balducci, 'Pianificazione strategica e politiche di sviluppo locale. Una relazione necessaria?', *Archivio di Studi Urbani e Regionali*, No. 64, 1999.

[9] P. Le Galès, 'Du gouvernment des villes à la gouvernance urbaine', *Revue Francaise de Science Politique*, 45(1), 1995, pp. 57–95.

generated Wikinomics,[10] which, following the advent of Web 2.0, have become Socialnomics,[11] where citizens are voluntary sensors.[12] Why the spontaneous action of citizens cannot be exploited to support programming in a sort of 'People-driven economy'? Why are several donations and free time of software specialists the most serious threat for Microsoft? And why a participatory approach to planning cannot in any way limit the power of real estate cartels in our cities? Why did hundreds of people Twit for months, composing the first social opera 'Twitter Dammerung' staged at the Royal Opera House in London and does no one think to adopt a Web 2.0 approach in spatial decision-making?[13]

These questions were taken into account in Marmo Platano–Melandro Territorial Integrated Projects (PITs). Marmo Platano–Melandro is an area with high potential in the north-western part of Basilicata Region (Italy), including 15 municipalities and two consortiums of communes in mountain areas. PITs are local organizations responsible for the accomplishment of Regional Operational Programs (POR) in Italian Objective 1 regions and for the elaboration of common and shared strategies for local development. Their major objective was the development of synergies and scale economies in a multi-scalar perspective of governance favouring groups of municipalities. Unfortunately, without any doubt, PITs represent a big missed opportunity to apply strategic planning principles, as political and bureaucratic obstacles transformed an instrument with great potential in a simple sum of projects proposed by municipalities without any form of evaluation.[14] Participatory and visioning phases were completely ignored, though the programme spanned for five years, and the analytical phase, in most cases, represented a sort of justification for already decided interventions.

In such a scenario, Marmo Platano–Melandro PIT might definitely be considered as an exception. A methodology of spatialization of programmed interventions has been developed, allowing, through the implementation of WEBSITE (a website providing to the citizens information on these interventions) and WEBGIS (a Geographic Information System on the Web), to increase the level of transparency concerning programming choices in the implementation phase. WEBGIS was coupled with a BLOG (a typical web log) providing interaction capabilities), in order to have feedback from citizens concerning the programmed interventions and taking an active part in defining the next programming phase.[15] In most of the current programming tools,

---

[10] D. Tapscott and A. D. Williams, *Wikinomics: How Mass Collaboration Changes Everything*, Penguin Group, New York, 2006.

[11] E. Qualman, *Socialnomics: How Social Media Transforms the Way we Live and do Business*, John Wiley, Hoboken, NJ, 2009.

[12] M. F. Goodchild, 'Citizens as sensors: the world of volunteered geography', *GeoJournal*, 69, 2007, pp. 211–221.

[13] C. Rinner, C. Keßler and S. Andrulis, 'The use of Web 2.0 concepts to support deliberation in spatial decision-making', *Computers, Environment and Urban Systems*, 32(5), 2008, pp. 386–395.

[14] F. D. Moccia, 'Resistenze alla pianificazione strategica: un'analisi trans-culturale della ricezione ed uso della pianificazione strategica nella pianificazione integrata italiana', in F. Archibugi and A. Saturnino (eds), *Pianificazione strategica e governabilità ambientale*, Alinea, Firenze, 2004.

[15] L. Tilio, F. Scorza, V. Lanza and B. Murgante, 'Open source resources and Web 2.0 potentialities for a new democratic approach in programming practices', *Lecture Notes in Artificial Intelligence*, Vol. 5736, Springer-Verlag, Berlin, 2009, pp. 228–237.

a bottom-up approach considers municipalities as the lowest level of shared decision, ignoring citizen knowledge, ideas, opinions and imagination, which might improve the quality of planning choices. In order to increase the extent of public participation, the above-mentioned systems, WEBSITE, WEBGIS and BLOG, inform people, promoting transparency in choices, and allow them to freely express their ideas and opinions, thus providing local authorities with the possibility to collect and use valuable knowledge.

The attempt of creating a new governance model, based on cohesion and cooperation among local authorities, is the way towards the improvement of efficacy and effectiveness. In this direction, major objectives of the experience described in this paper are:

(1) creating a common, extended and shared knowledge of territory;
(2) innovating programming procedures using geographical dimensions;
(3) making it possible to assess efficacy and effectiveness in public policies;
(4) increasing citizen participation for the EU programming period 2007–13, considering the lessons learned from 2000 to 2006 EU regional policies.

Programming Documents and Spatial Information

During the past decades, the main problem in GIS implementation was the lack of spatial data. Nowadays, the wide diffusion of electronic devices containing geo-referenced information has resulted in the production of extensive spatial data. This trend has led to 'GIS wikification',[16] where mass collaboration plays a key role in the main components of spatial information (hardware, software, data and people). The need of greater computing power (hardware) has been solved by grid computing; open source software has significantly increased market share. Mass collaboration in many cases represents a threat for a lot of professions and new terms have been coined, such as citizen journalism, citizen science, citizen geography, etc.[17] The term 'neogeography'[18] is often adopted to describe people activities when using and creating their own maps, geo-tagging pictures, movies, websites, etc.[19] It could be defined as a new approach to geography without a geographer.[20] Considering that this activity is mainly developed by enthusiasts, it is possible to reach good levels of accuracy in the same way that Wikipedia has reached quality levels comparable to *Encyclopaedia Britannica*.[21] The volunteered approach has been adopted by important American organizations, such as US Geological Survey, US Census Bureau, etc.

---

[16] D. S. Sui, 'The wikification of GIS and its consequences: or Angelina Jolie's new tattoo and the future of GIS', *Computers, Environment and Urban Systems*, 32(1), 2008, pp. 1–5.

[17] M. F. Goodchild, 'Citizens as voluntary sensors: spatial data infrastructure in the world of Web 2.0', *International Journal of Spatial Data Infrastructures Research*, 2, 2007, pp. 24–32.

[18] A. Turner, *Introduction to Neogeography*, O'Reilly Media, Sebastopol, CA, 2006.

[19] A. Hudson-Smith, R. Milton, J. Dearden and M. Batty, 'The neogeography of virtual cities: digital mirrors into a recursive world', in M. Foth, *Handbook of Research on Urban Informatics: The Practice and Promise of the Real-Time City*, Information Science Reference, IGI Global, Hershey, PA, 2009.

[20] M. F. Goodchild, 'NeoGeography and the nature of geographic expertise', *Journal of Location Based Services*, 3, 2009, pp. 82–96.

[21] J. Giles, 'Internet encyclopedias go head to head', *Nature*, 438, 2005, pp. 900–901.

Volunteered geographic information activities (e.g. Wikimapia, OpenStreetMap), public initiatives (e.g. Spatial Data Infrastructures, Geo-portals) and private projects (e.g. Google Earth, Microsoft Virtual Earth, etc.) produced an overabundance of spatial data.[22] Whilst technologies (e.g. GPS, remote sensing, etc.) can be useful in producing new spatial data, volunteered activities are the only way to update and describe such data. If, on the one hand, spatial data have been produced in various ways, on the other hand remote sensing, sensor networks and other electronic devices generate a great flow of geographically referenced data concerning diverse aspects of human activities or environmental phenomena monitoring.

Kitsuregawa et al.[23] called this era the 'Information-Explosion Era' since it is characterized by a large amount of information produced by human activities and automated systems; the capturing and manipulation of this information is called ubiquitous computing and represents a sort of bridge between computers and the real world, accounting for the social dimension of human environments.[24] If this technological evolution produced a new Paradigm of Urban Development, called u-City[25] in rural areas, like much of the Marmo Platano–Meladro area is, new approaches based on integration of Web 2.0 and spatial information could help local communities in pursuing the objectives of economic growth, considering sustainability and transparency in decision-making. In this scenario it is fundamental to develop a new method of spatialization for programming documents. These documents are not strictly connected to cartographic representations and the geographical description is vague in nature.[26] For this reason an attempt to translate policy statements into their geographical elements has been developed, establishing a method for the spatialization of economic programmes in order to increase efficiency and effectiveness of strategic actions (Figure 1). Another important activity was to implement the entire planning system in a GIS environment, governing the whole territory of the study area.

Local authorities are regulated by a huge number of plans developed over time, for a variety of purposes and at different scales. In most recent cases, local plans do not take into account sector-based plans, sometimes developing conflicting objectives. The use of GIS allows a synchronized interpretation of the planning system evaluating the conflicts with programming documents.

The spatialization of policy documents can be intended as a relevant contribution to the improvement of rationality in planning processes. In planning

---

[22] B. Murgante, G. Borruso and A. Lapucci, 'Geocomputation and urban planning', in B. Murgante, G. Borruso and A. Lapucci (eds), *Geocomputation and Urban Planning Studies in Computational Intelligence*, Vol. 176, Springer-Verlag, Berlin, 2009, pp. 1–18.

[23] M. Kitsuregawa, S. Matsuoka, T. Matsuyama, O. Sudoh and J. Adachi, 'Cyber infrastructure for the information-explosion era', *Journal of Japanese Society for Artificial Intelligence*, 22(2), 2007, pp. 209–214.

[24] A. Greenfeld and M. Shepard, *Urban Computing and Its Discontents*, The Architectural League of New York, 2007.

[25] J. S. Hwang, 'u-City: the next paradigm of urban development', in M. Foth, *Handbook of Research on Urban Informatics: The Practice and Promise of the Real-Time City*, Information Science Reference, IGI Global, Hershey, PA, 2009.

[26] H. Ottens, 'An information model for strategic spatial policy documents', *Proceedings of the Seventh Agile International Conference on Geographical Information Science*, Heraklion, 2004.

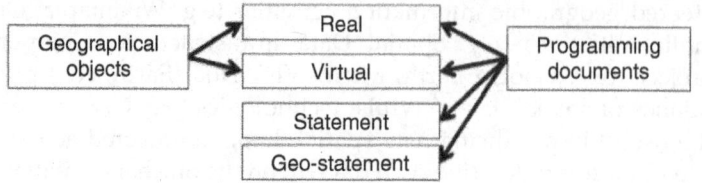

Figure 1. Programming documents and geographical information.

theory, there is a general agreement in these seven requirements for the rationality of strategic planning:[27]

(1) a better knowledge coherent with management objectives;
(2) a better knowledge of resources in order to choose more appropriate and effective means for achieving objectives;
(3) a better knowledge of the complete effects and impacts of decisions;
(4) a better knowledge of the compatibility of decisions with other decisions by the same decisional subject;
(5) a better knowledge of the compatibility of decisions with other decisions by subjects which operate in the same field;
(6) a better knowledge of costs and direct results involved in subject decisions;
(7) a better ability to estimate relationships between costs and results (agreed as effects in comparison with objectives).

The term 'knowledge' appears almost in all these seven statements. The possibility to analyse strategic documents also according to geographical components must be considered as a huge increase of knowledge. For instance, the third statement may allow a better external effect evaluation in spatial terms. Points 4 and 5 highlight coherence, compatibility, redundancy and duplication. Some assessment ambiguities might occur in analysing strategic documents only considering the agency or organization promoting them. Spatial aspects may allow us to recognize in advance redundancies generated by geographical proximity of some programmes developed from different local authorities.

In this project, we did not limit our analysis to the socio-economic framework. We worked to identify the exact location of interventions produced on the context by programmes and plans. Inspections and interviews with local managers have been carried out in order to define a local intervention framework. A preliminary study of programming documents has been carried out with the aim of achieving an effective synthesis of major contents, trying to homogenize information which is different in each document and at a different scale.

On the one hand, this activity has allowed us to carry out a first evaluation concerning the degree of coherence between actions and vocations, potentialities and specific expectations of the territorial context; on the other hand, it has allowed us to verify the coherence between choices of socio-economic programming. Representation of interventions by means of geometric primitives has been addressed in the following way (Figure 2):

---

[27] F. Archibugi, *Introduction to Strategic Planning in the Public Domain*, Planning Studies Centre, Rome, 2002.

(1) *localized and georeferenced interventions*: geographical data have been located on the intervention object, or on the whole of the indications of infrastructures for mobility routes;
(2) *localized and not georeferenced interventions*: geographical data have been located on specific territorial boundaries (e.g. downtowns, industrial areas, census zones), or, in the case of linear data with unknown path intervention, they can be represented by a simple line connecting the interested zones;
(3) *neither localized nor georeferenced interventions*: geographical data do not fit this kind of intervention because they are intrinsically not localized (education programmes), or, in some cases, can be referred to administrative boundaries (e.g. Regions, Provinces, Municipalities).

Spatialization concerns several informative layers, mostly related to economic programming, more particularly POR interventions, infrastructural interventions funded by PIT and State aids during the same programming period, but also some other services and elements, linked to the rural system, as farms, tourist services, handmade productions, etc. As mentioned above, one of the weaknesses of programming documents is vagueness of geographical location. Difficulties in the localization phase are mainly related to the great amount of elements to locate and to the lack of related information. Two approaches have been pursued: many activities have been located on maps using the local knowledge of municipality staff who were able to identify precise intervention positions; the remaining interventions have been identified by means of Google Earth. This approach could increase the transparency of choices, in the programming phase evaluation, assessing interventions in their context, analysing spatial location and obtaining a measure of *ex ante* coherence and *ex post* efficacy of the context. The spatialization procedure may increase the level of efficacy and efficiency, because it is possible to compare programming to planning documents, constraint systems and territorial features in a very detailed way.

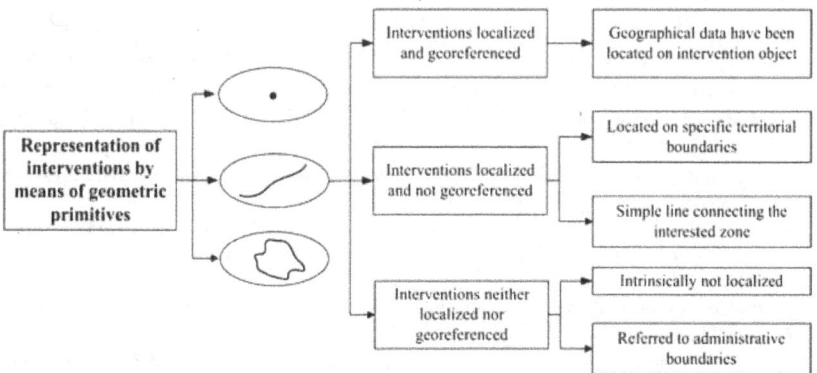

Figure 2. Spatialization of programming documents scheme.

An E-approach for Programming Activities: Web 2.0 Tools for PIT

In recent years, the Internet has become a popular medium for carrying out all kinds of commercial, social and governmental activities. Presumably it has become a part of society quicker than any other new technology and it is now considered as a new democratizing tool, supposedly bringing people closer together and allowing them to participate in social and political activity.[28] During the last decade, all governments and local organizations have been using the Internet and ICT e-government tools more and more in order to give more opportunities for citizen participation and therefore for enhancing information and service delivery to citizens. It is necessary to consider that citizen participation needs constant communication, using new tools in order to facilitate a bottom-up participation process.[29] It is also important that, especially at this time and in this society, citizens perceive that their actions could be appreciated and partially or totally accepted by local authorities. This approach offers the advantage of stimulating citizen involvement in the choice of design alternatives in programming processes, overcoming time and space constraints.

According to a study led by Evans-Cowley and Conroy examining municipal planning-related US websites, we can distinguish between two types of electronic tools: information tools, representing a low participation level and providing a 'one-way' participation, and interaction tools, providing a 'two-way' participation, including citizens' opinions, considering them as process actors through a mutual exchange of comments, questions, discussion channels, etc.[30]

Taking these into account in Marmo Platano–Melandro a typical information provision tool, named WEBSITE, was developed, which contains news, information from press reviews, events, publications, invitations and notices, documents and sections aiming to explain PIT objectives, principles and implementation status, institutional activities, projects, photos and videos. Unfortunately, at present, WEBSITE (www.pitmpm.it) is not available, due to changes in local administration.

Although it is a very popular communication tool among governments and institutions, and despite the fact that the Marmo Platano–Melandro PIT WEBSITE is very complete in content and information, it represents a low participation level. In order to achieve a higher participation level, an interaction tool, the WEBGIS, has been activated to generate a distributed and collaborative environment.[31] It can be defined as an 'interactive information tool', since on the one hand it gives geographic information and allows every stakeholder to be informed about the territory. On the other hand, indeed, the user has to decide what kind of information he/she wants to receive, what reference scale and

---

[28] S. Woolgar (ed.), *Virtual Society?—Technology, Cyberbole, Reality,* Oxford University Press, Oxford, 2002.

[29] S. Knapp and V. Coors, 'The use of eParticipation systems in public participation: the VEPs example', in V. Coors *et al.* (eds), *Urban and Regional Data Management,* Taylor and Francis, London, 2008, pp. 93–104.

[30] J. Evans-Cowley and M. M. Conroy, 'The growth of e-government in municipal planning', *Journal of Urban Technology,* 13(1), 2006, pp. 81–107.

[31] S. Boroushaki and J. Malczewski, 'ParcitipatoryGIS.com: a WebGIS-based collaborative multicriteria decision analysis', *Journal of the Urban and Regional Information Systems Association,* 22(1), 2010, pp. 23–32.

detail level he/she wants to reach; so there is a sort of interaction with the WEBGIS.

However, WEBSITE and WEBGIS are not enough for public participation as the information flow goes only from PIT to citizens. It is important to create a kind of virtual space where people can discuss, compare and exchange information, suggesting ideas to public administrations. The support of Web 2.0 (the new emerging model of the Internet, based on extensive content generation by users and collaboration) and ICT technologies aims to capitalize collective intelligence in programming processes. Interesting aspects are related, on the one hand, to the creation of a real local organization network, in order to promote transparency, participation to choices, equity, redistribution principles and, on the other hand, to the application of ICT new tools to promote citizen participation in community activities.

Theories about communicative planning have emphasized forcefully how language and modes of communication play a key role in shaping planning practices, public dialogues, policy-making and collaboration processes,[32] and today the most popular and effective tool for exchanging opinions and collecting information is the web log (blog). So, it has been decided to use a BLOG as an interaction tool, since other tools (e.g. e-mail addresses) on the one hand definitely give citizens a different way to communicate their ideas, questions and concerns, and on the other hand do not allow the planner or any management planning or programming process to assure transparency and sharing. Later on, specific attention is dedicated to two of the electronic tools used: WEBGIS and BLOG.

In order to promote a spread of spatial data knowledge, allow consultation of planning and programming documents, involve different stakeholders' participation and increase the transparency level of programming choices via the Internet, this research project led to two main concrete results, a WEBGIS and a Web Map Service.[33]

According to the opinion of the administration, the above-mentioned objectives are considered strategic to achieving its key objectives of promoting local development and adopting new governance models. Spatial data knowledge contributes to improve rationality in planning processes, so that acquisition and production of spatial information have been important phases of research; but once data have been collected and produced, the next important issue is how to make information available for citizens and stakeholders. The Internet, and especially web-based GIS systems, can be the means to promote open accessibility and effective distribution of spatial information.[34]

Also considering that several administrations act on the Marmo Platano–Melandro area and that they use spatial information (moreover, they contribute to data acquisition and production), it seemed interesting to adopt the INSPIRE directive and work to realize a spatial data infrastructure. Due to scarcity of resources and a low GIS culture, the attempt was really hard, so that at the

---

[32] J. Pløger, 'Public participation and the art of governance', *Environment and Planning B: Planning and Design*, 28, 2001, pp. 219–241.

[33] Available respectively at: <www.pitmpm.basilicata.it/PIT/map.phtml> and <www.pitmpm.basilicata.it/cgi-bin/wms_pit>

[34] Boroushaki and Malczewski, op. cit.

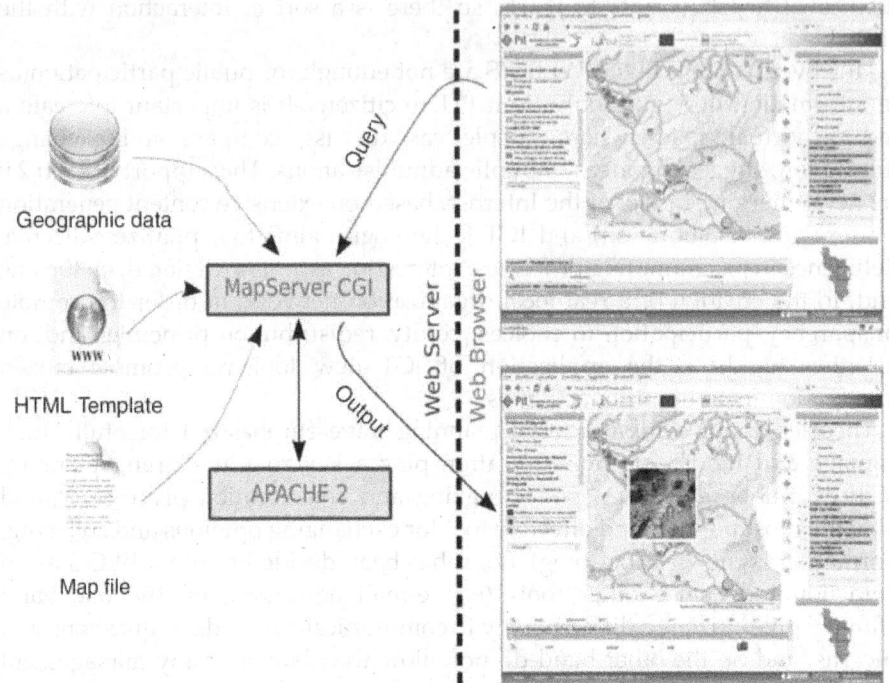

Figure 3. Marmo Platano–Melandro PIT WEBGIS architecture.

moment PIT has not yet completed its own Spatial Data Infrastructure, but it is working towards it. At present, as mentioned above, two concrete tools have been implemented, which are useful for objective fulfilment: WEBGIS and WMS.

WEBGIS, implemented on an open-source platform, is based on a client-server architecture which accesses rules via Internet or intranet in order to navigate, update and maintain data; its architecture is shown in Figure 3. The adopted operating system is Debian GNU/Linux, and the most common applications of Geospatial Free and Open Source Software (GFOSS) have been used. Open GIS Consortium specifications have been adopted, in order to ensure interchange and interoperability standards for WEBGIS systems, and each informative layer is provided with metadata, edited according to ISO 19115 standard and following Metadata National Repertory (CNIPA). WEBGIS has been created so that three kinds of users can login, in order to participate in consultations: citizens and non-expert users, local administration and finally PIT administrators.

Concerning content, it is possible to divide it into four groups of informative layers:

(1) Basic Data Layers: this group includes data layers concerning territorial structures: administrative limits, road and railway network, hydrography, etc.;
(2) Socio-Economical Data Layers: in this group information concerning population and employment characteristics of the area is included;
(3) Planning System and Constraint System Data Layers: urban plans and sector-based plans, after homogenization, are included in this group;

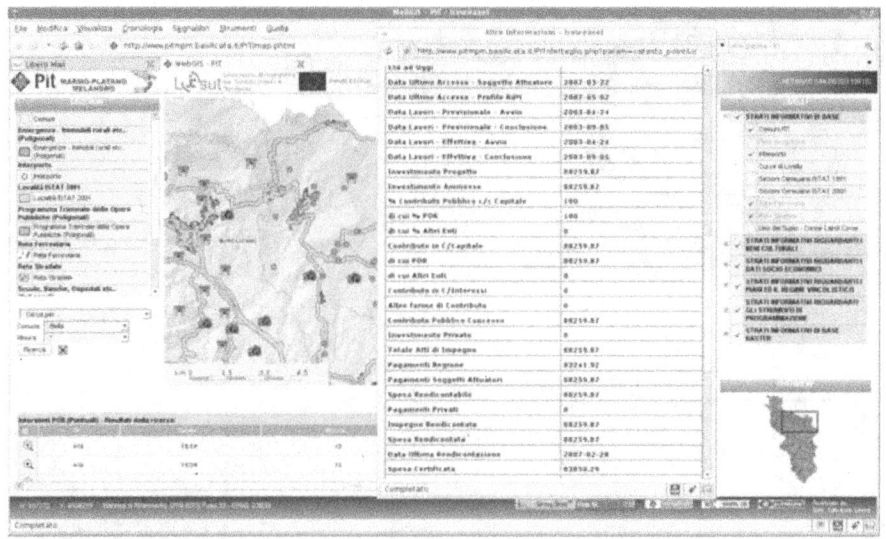

Figure 4. Marmo Platano–Melandro PIT WEBGIS (http://www.pitmpm.basilicata.it/PIT/map.phtml).

(4) Economic Programming Data Layers: this group includes information on programming documents concerning POR Basilicata 2000–2006, socio-economic plan of consortium of communes in mountain areas and other economic programming documents. These data have been produced, introducing an important innovation concerning spatialization of economic documents, that typically miss the spatial dimension as mentioned above.

Concerning available tools, WEBGIS allows citizens, practitioners and employees to navigate choosing/selecting in a very simple way (its interface is completely user-friendly), visualizing spatial data, zooming on a specific area and also interrogating the system. This capability to submit queries in this context represents a great contribution to increasing transparency of practices and procedures. In fact, it is possible to obtain information concerning interventions of economic programmes, in terms of expenditure. Citizens, surfing in WEBGIS, can become aware that in their municipality a certain amount of public funds have been spent in local development interventions. The screenshot of Figure 4 shows an example of such a query, with results in a pop-up.

According to the OGC standard, in order to improve the spread of spatial data information, a Web Map Service (WMS) has been implemented, that is a standard and free service through which it is possible dynamically to reproduce maps, visualized as JPEG, GIF or PNG in any GIS software. Users, adding a URL, could overlap other data to their own data. The Web Map Service is available at the URL www.pitmpm.basilicata.it/cgi-bin/wms_pit.

In Macpherson's study[35] different kinds of such tools were listed among interaction tools. Interaction tools include e-mail addresses for e-mailing questions, online registration for news and other information, online application

---

[35] L. Macpherson, 'Joystick not included: new media technologies are ideal tools for gaining stakeholder interest, acceptance', *Water Environment and Technology*, 11(9), 1999, pp. 51–53.

E-PARTICIPATION IN SOUTHERN EUROPE AND THE BALKANS

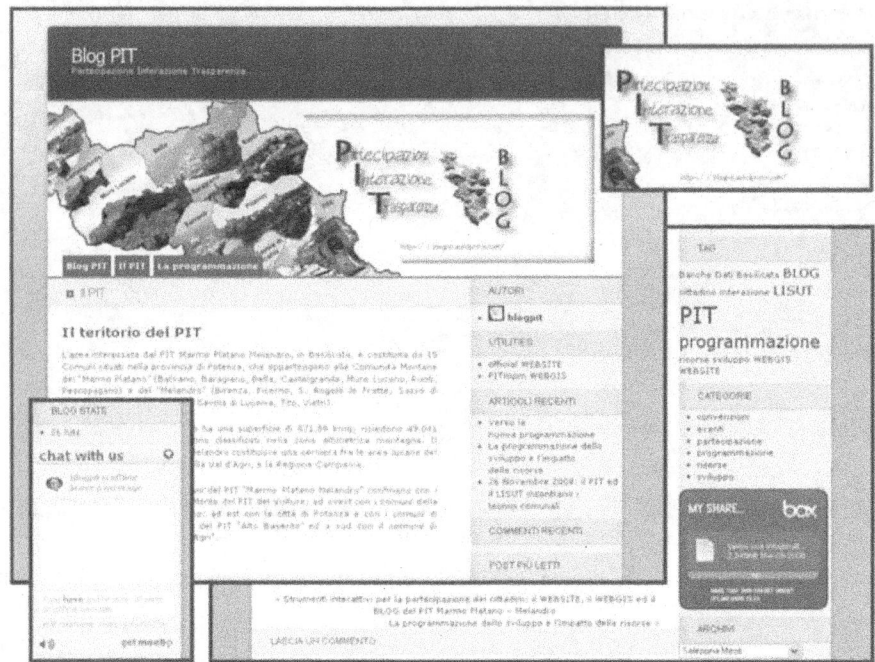

Figure 5. Marmo Platano–Melandro PIT BLOG (http://BLOGpit.wordpress.com).

submissions and online planning discussion forums. In our case a set of e-tools has been developed, considering different kinds of communication possible via the Internet, in the firm belief that the great potential of the Internet allows citizens to 'visualize issues and concepts, participate in dialogue, and gain knowledge by interacting'. The most suitable interaction tool for this experience is the blog. The BLOG[36] (Figure 5) designed for the Marmo Platano–Melandro PIT derives from the need to ensure citizens' information and interaction with the institutions on government policies.

BLOG purposes can be summarized in the following points:

(1) active participation of users through comments;
(2) collection of all instances concerning past and future programming policies;
(3) dialogue between organizations and data users;
(4) collaboration relationship and constant involvement of citizens in public decisions;
(5) transparency and accessibility to decision-making processes;
(6) transparency in intervention programming.

The BLOG represents a resource for local development, community life and identity; it promotes collaborative relationships and constant citizen involvement in public decisions, overcoming typical participation constraints and giving more emphasis to the role of citizens. At present, we cannot give any interesting result concerning the use of the BLOG because it has been available only for a short time. At present it is not available, due to changes in local administration, but we

---

[36] Available at: <http://blogpit.wordpress.com>.

hope that it will again be online from September 2010, in order to guarantee a real citizenship involvement into the 2007–13 programming period.

Interoperability in E-government Process: New Issues in Organizing and Sharing Knowledge

This complex framework of e-tools for bottom-up public participation processes, concerning programming and management of local development, poses several issues related to common problems of participation processes, which are primarily connected to the procedural structure considered at the base of EU Regional Policies and Funds. Do stakeholders understand the meaning of general and sectoral policies? Are citizens aware of technical instruments implementing such policies? Are they conscious of *ex ante* comprehensive context analysis and/or can they share possible future scenarios? The system of knowledge connected to planning tools is mainly interdisciplinary and involves a lot of technical interventions. Each technical field of knowledge implies different languages, different regulations, different axioms, etc. Thus the planner has to manage a multidisciplinary complexity with the heavy task of communication and interaction with the decisional levels (mainly the political one) and with the hierarchy of participatory levels defined by laws and by the new practices of bottom-up planning. This complex system of interactions could effectively work under the assumption of a distributed and shared knowledge among the actors participating in the process. In practice it is possible to demonstrate how difficult it is to realize such a condition. On the basis of these considerations it is possible to identify two methodological hypotheses: (i) citizens (or actors) involved in the process hold the complete technical/scientific knowledge of disciplines concerning the planning process; (ii) there is a strong direction (the 'planning office' or similar structure involving the planner) entitled to manage the process. Among others, a task to be accomplished is to interpret 'common' requests, often points of view, expressed by those citizens as technical views.

The second hypothesis implies a process of reinterpretation and translation with the risk of personal interpretation of the issues promoted by participants. It could affect the bottom-up approach and the whole rationality of the planning process. Generally speaking, the first hypothesis could be defined as an absurd condition even if it fully guarantees the bottom-up approach in a framework of wide participation of actors, stakeholders and beneficiaries. But if we design a bounded participation for the planning process we could consider the first hypothesis as verified. We intend that the participant community should be restricted to a number of representative bodies with technical competences able to manage and interact with the planner and the decisional level of the process.

It is possible to identify the following critical factors: (i) open participation processes must be managed by effective groups of experts (previously defined as 'strong direction') but this could cause a problem of personal interpretation of instances produced by the bottom-up process; (ii) restricted participation should ensure representativeness of involved actors in order to get relevant results in the planning process; (iii) an over-tasked 'strong direction' (responsible for the technical development of the plan and for the participation management) could be ineffective without concrete opportunities to produce the expected results.

The key problem in enlarging participation appears to be related to a difficulty of communication between involved actors in accordance with the general assumption by Uschold and Gruninger: 'people organizations and software systems must communicate among themselves. [...] there can be widely varying viewpoints and assumptions regarding the same subject matter.'[37] In this 'lacking shared understanding' framework, the level of communication decreases and consequently, interaction between actors becomes ineffective even if supported by e-tools. In defining a programme, this misunderstanding participation could cause difficulties concerning the identification of objectives and priorities with subsequent problems related to the decisional level. The comparison with interoperability in spatial data infrastructures (referring to Pundt,[38] Mark et al.,[39] Lemmens et al.[40] and Fonseca[41]) should be considered as well.

Starting from the definition by Laurini and Murgante,[42] we might affirm that, in our context interoperability is the 'technical incapacity for different systems, actors or stakeholders to work together without conflicts in procedures or contents'. According to this definition, 'systems' include normative tools, regulations, laws, other plans or programmes overseeing the planning process.

Therefore, new problems coming from the implementation of e-tools in programming local development are closely connected to the level of sharing knowledge in technical understanding (including interdisciplinary, normative and procedural issues) and in contents. One way to tackle such problems is the use of ontologies. Overcoming the traditional philosophical definition of ontology as the 'discipline dealing with theories of being', we will use a slightly different notion of a specific ontology *as a model* which can be defined as *'the explicit specification of an abstract, simplified view of a world we desire to represent'* (proposed, among others, by Gruber[43]).

Structural elements of the ontology are: domain (or 'scope' of the ontology), concepts ('classes'), hierarchies, attributes of concepts, restrictions and relations between concepts, instances. The definition of such elements represents the 'ontology design'.[44] The domain is the abstraction of the reality we want to represent and, in the study case, it is composed of physical elements, relations between them, value systems, programme actions, social issues and policy goals. The ontological representation aims to obtain a greater efficacy in the

---

[37] M. Uschold and M. Gruninger, 'Ontologies: principles, methods and applications', *Knowledge Engineering Review*, 11, 1996, pp. 36–116.

[38] H. Pundt, 'Domain ontologies for data sharing—an example from environmental monitoring using field GIS', *Computers & Geosciences*, 28(1), 2002, pp. 95–102, doi:10.1016/S0098-3004(01)00018-8.

[39] D. M. Mark, B. Smith and B. Tversky, 'Ontology and geographic objects: an empirical study of cognitive categorization', *Cognitive Science*, 1997.

[40] R. Lemmens, M. de Vries and T. Aditya, 'Semantic extension of GEO WEB service descriptions with ontology languages', *Proceedings of the 6th AGILE*, Vol. 1, Lyon, 2003.

[41] F. Fonseca, 'Ontologies and knowledge sharing in urban GIS', *Computers, Environment and Urban Systems*, 24(3), 2000, pp. 251–272, doi:10.1016/S0198-9715(00)00004-1.

[42] R. Laurini and B. Murgante, 'Interoperabilità semantica e geometrica nelle basi di dati geografiche nella pianificazione urbana', in B. Murgante (ed.), *L'informazione geografica a supporto della pianificazione territoriale*, Franco Angeli, Milano, 2008, pp. 229–244.

[43] T. R. Gruber, 'Toward principles for the design of ontologies used for knowledge sharing', *International Journal of Human and Computer Studies*, 43(5/6), 1995, pp. 907–928.

[44] P. Ceravolo and E. Damiani, 'Introduction to ontology engineering', in A. Zilli et al. (eds), *Semantic Knowledge Management: An Ontology-Based Framework*, Information Science Reference, IGI Global, Hershey, PA, 2008, ISBN 978-1-60566-034-9.

participation process overcoming the traditional collection of 'people's points of view' in order to gain a real bottom-up process in programming local development.

Ontology may have different formalizations and must necessarily include a thesaurus of terms (concept names) and associated definitions (axioms), and (at least) taxonomic relationships. In an ontological system, a 'concept' is an accurate representation of an entity belonging to the reality. Entities can be 'real' or 'abstract'. Concepts can be linked by taxonomic relations and non-taxonomic relations and may be defined by axioms expressible in natural language, logical or procedural formalization.

Among others, Garro and Ruffolo[45] precise that taxonomic relations, through which one can build hierarchies and/or taxonomies of concepts, are expressed through the following two constructs:

(1) specialization and/or generalization (IS_A);
(2) part-of and/or compound-of (PART_OF, HAS_PART).

An example of non-taxonomic relation between concepts is the 'similarity', which specifies the degree of similarity between different concepts through a similarity coefficient.

Axiomatic relations, in other words the assumptions on the concepts and their relations, are expressible through:

(1) strong constraints, which specify absolutely necessary conditions for a concept in order to express a certain property;
(2) weak constraints, which specify the conditions that would be preferable to occur so that a given concept could express a certain property.

Intrinsic properties of ontological entities are specified through the following two types of properties or attributes:

(1) unstructured properties or attributes specifying characteristics expressed through natural language;
(2) structured properties or attributes specifying a characteristic expressed in a precise representation formalism (for instance, a portion of the diagram entities/relations).

Different examples of ontologies are accessible in several scientific areas. Loukis[46] analysed several examples of existing ontologies in the field of public policy-making. Among the existing sectoral ontologies (e.g. for the environment, cultural heritage, government, etc.) problems of interaction among actors involved in the process are not fully addressed. In fact, several ontologies are mainly glossaries of terms regarding a specific knowledge sector. Other examples concern very specific applications with limited opportunities to be transferred in other contexts. In the field of planning, a relevant example is PLANET

---

[45] A. Garro and M. Ruffolo, 'Gestire la Conoscenza in Domini Complessi: Rappresentazione e Gestione di Ontologie attraverso Mappe della Conoscenza (Knowledge Map)', Rapporto Tecnico ICAR/CS/2003/03, ICAR-CNR—Istituto di Calcolo e Reti ad Alte Prestazioni del Consiglio Nazionale delle Ricerche, 2003.

[46] E. Loukis, 'An ontology for G2G collaboration in public policy making, implementation and evaluation', *Artificial Intelligence and Law*, 15(1), 2007, pp. 19–48.

Ontology,[47] but for our research purposes no sources were available. In fact, the case of PLANET application concerns the representation of territorial and urban plans without integration with the level of programming economic resources for local development, too. Therefore, a process of ontology building has been developed following instances that emerged from e-tools design and implementation. Results belong to the class of 'Domain ontologies' as described in the classification proposed by Visser and Bench-Capon.[48]

In this case we structured our ontology including the following super-classes:

(1) Plan, defined as 'Written account of intended future course of action (scheme), aiming at achieving specific goal(s) or objective(s) within a specific timeframe. It explains in a detailed way what, when, how, and by whom the work needs to be done and often it includes best case, expected case, and worst case scenarios.'[49]
(2) Project, defined as 'Planned set of interrelated tasks to be executed over a fixed period and within certain costs and other limitations.'[50]
(3) Policy, defined as 'A specific statement of principle or of guiding actions that implies clear commitment but is not mandatory. A general direction that a governmental agency sets to follow, in order to meet its goals and objectives before undertaking an action program.'[51]
(4) Tools, defined as 'Financial or normative instruments for policy implementation' (our definition).
(5) Actors, defined as 'Groups of private, public, no-profit bodies involved in development process' (our definition).

Figure 6 represents the super-classes structure of our ontology with the main relations among them.

In order to be useful, the ontology has to be shared. In an international community of users, the first difficulty comes from languages, but a similar problem emerges when we match together different programmes or plans adopted by different bodies. Ontologies can help the community to define and make explicit a common language and strengthen the efficacy of direct interactions.

The development of an ontology might be quite different depending on the level of users' involvement. In the present case, the ontological approach has been developed by a limited group of experts (managing the research project, coming from different scientific disciplines). The result is an ontology that will be 'imposed' on the community members through the above-mentioned e-tools (WEBSITE, WEBGIS, BLOG). Following an agreed building process among

---

[47] Y. Gil and J. Blythe, 'PLANET: a shareable and reusable ontology for representing plans', in *AAAI Workshop on Representational Issues for Real-World Planning Systems*, 2000, available at: <http://scholar.google.com/scholar?hl=en&btnG=Search&q=intitle:PLANET:+A+Shareable+and+Reusable+Ontology+for+Representing+Plans#0> (accessed February 2011).

[48] P. R. S. Visser and T. J. M. Bench-Capon, 'On the reusability of ontologies in knowledge systems design', in *The Proceedings of the Seventh International Workshop on Database and Expert Systems Applications—DEXA '96*, Zurich, Switzerland, 1996, pp. 256–261.

[49] Business Dictionary, available at: <http://www.businessdictionary.com/>.

[50] Business Dictionary, available at: <http://www.businessdictionary.com/>.

[51] N. H. Knox, with the contribution of L. Mintier, 'The California general plan glossary', in C. H. Knox and N. H. Knox (eds), *California Planning Roundtable*, June 2003, available at: <http://www.cproundtable.org/publications/california-general-plan-glossary/> (accessed February 2011).

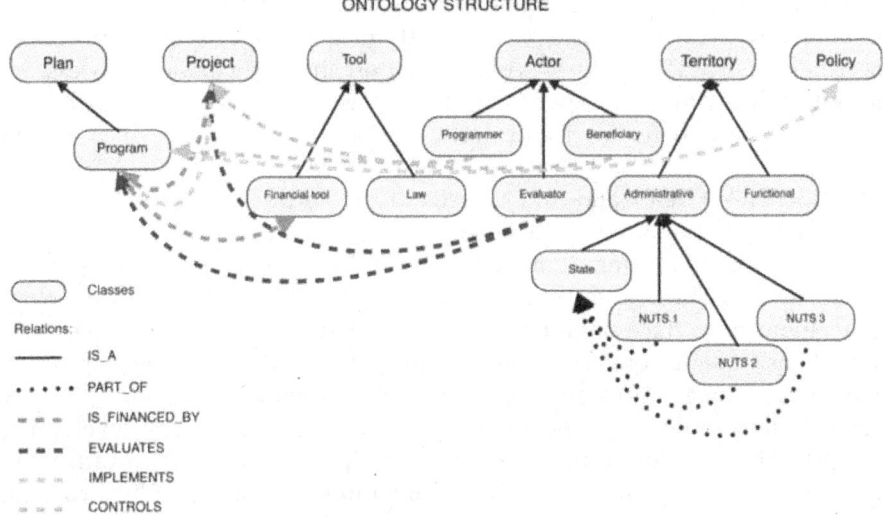

Figure 6. Ontology structure.

experts, a kind of negotiation process of class identification and axiom selection, we developed a thesaurus of 183 terms and, at the end of the process, we obtained a complex network of classes and relations including: 124 classes, 148 axioms and 11 independent relations. This is still considered an ongoing tool because of the nature of the domain of the application, but it is ready to be adopted in the framework of the new EU programming period 2007–13.

Conclusions

In the framework of reticular strategic governance processes, the adoption of an e-tools system supporting public participation represents an innovative experience, considering both the domain of the application and the methodological structure. However, enhancement of bottom-up processes based on public participation remains an exception in current practices, since the counterfactual case[52] is still an improbable assessment and too many resources are devoted to manage administrative procedures rather than to develop effective planning. The methodology we adopted in the case described in this paper merged together freeware ICT platforms and spatial data infrastructures in a brand new integrated system, aiming to improve the level of participation. Consequently the experience analysed in this research may be attributed to the 1990s visionary approach to strategic planning.

Generally, in an electronic environment, it is possible to establish a democratic place where everyone can freely express themselves. Moreover, electronic participation exceeds the typical limitations of traditional participation, as synchronous and location-based,[53] and it encourages individuals, who are in

---

[52] P. Bishop, T. Hart, P. Gripaios and E. McVittie, 'Analysing the impact of Objective 1 funding in Europe: a review', *Environmental and Planning C: Government and Policy*, 26, 2008, pp. 499–524.

[53] Boroushaki and Malczewski, op. cit.

general reluctant,[54] to express their preferences. In this way, the use of ICT represents a fruitful strategy for bottom-up programming processes. Nevertheless, if ICT tools improve and support the participation process, it is relevant to underline the importance of developing such a process based on a widely shared knowledge framework through the adoption of a domain ontology.

WEBSITE, WEBGIS and BLOG seem to be attractive tools to promote participatory practices among citizens, because they are becoming more and more familiar to them. Having 'familiar' tools might greatly increase potential 'participation'.[55] Through this integrated e-government system, we might obtain a transition from face-oriented or file-oriented governance services to a comprehensive digital one. This might result in increased effectiveness, improved public information diffusion and enhanced participation opportunities for citizens.[56] Innovative experiences of participation in planning development (established by local authorities) are still relatively rare. It is possible to affirm that our approach could provide effective means through which planners can fully engage with the communities they serve through a more informed planning process.[57]

In the so-called 'consensus logic', the PIT project aimed to build a way of informing and making stakeholders involved in programming processes. The perspective of this first achievement was to help citizens understand, interact and work with the programmers in reaching 'optimal' solutions. This scenario is useful if we consider the EU programming period 2007–13.

As mentioned before, in Italy during recent years few initiatives for citizen involvement in decisional processes have been taken and only a small part of them are described in the literature. In fact, participation processes are mainly applied in urban renewal and urban design experiences. Therefore, the Marmo Platano–Melandro PIT experience, considered as a little experiment, should be taken into account for its relevant and innovative participation aspect connected to local development programming. So it is useful to summarize the major achievements of this experience:

(1) the definition of an e-democratic approach oriented to improve participation in governance processes;
(2) the development of a complex integrated system of e-tools supporting participation management.

The enhancement of the assessment function in programming and managing EU resources could be an additional result of the process. Participants could express ongoing and final evaluations, as components of a comprehensive and

---

[54] P. Jankowski, 'Towards participatory geographical information systems for community-based environmental decision making', *Journal of Environmental Management*, 90, 2009, pp. 1966–1971.

[55] V. Lanza and D. Prosperi, 'Collaborative e-governance: describing and pre-calibrating the digital milieu', *Urban and Regional Data Management*, Taylor and Francis, London, 2009.

[56] M. M. Conroy and J. Evans-Cowley, 'E-participation in planning: an analysis of cities adopting on-line citizen participation tools', *Environment and Planning C: Government and Policy*, 24, 2006, pp. 371–384.

[57] M. Tewdwr-Jones and H. Thomas, 'Collaborative action in local plan-making: planners' perceptions of "planning through debate"', *Environment and Planning B: Planning and Design*, 25, 1998, pp. 127–144.

context-based evaluation approach,[58] since they hold the basic and necessary knowledge and they are aware of the objectives of the programme, so that they can recognize its direct and indirect impacts on the context.

Beniamino Murgante is Assistant Professor of Urban and Regional Planning at the University of Basilicata (Southern Italy). His main research interests are urban and regional planning with a focus on the use of spatial information for developing decision support systems based on multi-criteria evaluation, fuzzy sets, rough sets and geo-statistical methods.

Lucia Tilio is a PhD student in Sciences and Methods for European Cities and Territories in the Laboratory of Engineering of Urban and Territorial System at the University of Basilicata. Her main research topics are public decision processes and decision support systems.

Viviana Lanza is Postdoctoral Researcher at the University of Basilicata. She is interested in communicative and participative aspects of urban planning, and in particular in electronic participation in the planning process. She has also conducted research at the Florida Atlantic University, collaborating with Professor David Prosperi.

Francesco Scorza is a PhD student in Sciences and Methods for European Cities and Territories in the Laboratory of Engineering of Urban and Territorial System at the University of Basilicata. His main research topics are strategic planning and evaluation.

---

[58] G. Las Casas and F. Scorza, 'Comprehensive evaluation and context based approach for the future of Regional Operative Programming in Europe', *Proceedings of 48th European Regional Science Association Congress 2008*, Liverpool, 2008.

Participatory policy process design: lessons learned from three European regions

CLELIA COLOMBO, MATEJA KUNSTELJ, FRANCESCO MOLINARI and LJUPCO TODOROVSKI

Introduction

Electronic Participation (eParticipation) generally refers to the use of information and communication technologies (ICTs) to enhance people's activism and citizens' involvement in public affairs—with a particular emphasis on legislation and policy-making—of modern democratic societies. Recently, the fastest growth of both 'top-down' (i.e. Government-driven) and 'bottom-up' (i.e. spontaneously emerging from the citizenry) eParticipation experiments in Western Europe and elsewhere, has inspired a number of interpretive frameworks, which have been developed by several leading scholars, such as Anttiroiko,[1] Macintosh,[2] Tambouris et al.,[3] Kalampokis et al.,[4] Aichholzer and Westholm,[5] and Bicking and Wimmer,[6] with the aim of scoping, characterizing and evaluating this relatively new phenomenon and its reported impact on civic engagement, as well as on Public Administration's innovation.

Besides the ritual wish to improve voter turnout and stimulate new forms of active citizenship through the diffusion of ICTs, a common feature of the above frameworks is that they all focus on Public Administration processes—in the legislative, administrative or policy-making domains—as the natural 'loci' of deployment and implementation of eParticipation methods and tools, also compared with more traditional ('offline') participation. The reason is quite straightforward: even in its bottom-up instantiations, eParticipation is always

---

[1] A. V. Anttiroiko, 'Building strong e-democracy—the role of technology in developing democracy for the information age', *ACM Communications*, 46(9), September 2003.

[2] A. Macintosh, 'Characterizing e-Participation in policy-making', in *Proceedings of the 37th Hawaii International Conference on System Sciences*, 2004, available at: <http://csdl2.computer.org/comp/proceedings/hicss/2004/2056/05/205650117a.pdf> (accessed April 2008).

[3] E. Tambouris, N. Liotas and K. Tarabanis, 'A framework for assessing eParticipation projects and tools', in *Proceedings of the 40th Hawaii International Conference on System Sciences*, 2007; and E. Tambouris, N. Liotas, D. Kaliviotis and K. Tarabanis, 'A framework for scoping eParticipation', in *Proceedings of the 8th Annual International Digital Government Research Conference*, 2007.

[4] E. Kalampokis, E. Tambouris and K. Tarabanis, 'A domain model for eParticipation', in *Proceedings of the 3rd International Conference on Internet and Web Applications and Services*, 2008.

[5] G. Aichholzer and H. Westholm, 'Evaluating eParticipation projects: practical examples and outline of an evaluation framework', *European Journal of ePractice*, No. 7, March 2009. Available at: <http://www.epractice.eu> (accessed 14 December 2009).

[6] M. Bicking and M. Wimmer, 'Evaluation framework to assess eParticipation projects in Europe', in E. Tambouris and A. Macintosh (eds), *Proceedings of the ePART2009 Conference*, Trauner Verlag, Linz, 2009, pp. 67–75.

encompassed within some structured, or informal, way of interaction between Government and citizens, which can be more easily and clearly understood in the context of a process—usually, though not every time, a public decision-making process.

However, being more interested in characterizing eParticipation projects per se, the above strand of literature does not dedicate a comparable effort in locating and modelling the specific Public Administration processes that are affected by them. As an example, Tambouris et al.[7] introduce five main layers for the categorization of eParticipation, the first of which—they call 'democratic processes'—reportedly includes broadly defined activities such as 'voting, campaigning, campaign financing, public debate and discussion, civics education, and processes within and between political parties, grassroots organisations, information intermediaries and communication between policy makers and the public'. Going one level down, as shown in Figure 1, Tambouris et al.[8] locate the policy-making cycle first defined by Anttiroiko[9] and then by Macintosh[10]—based on the five stages of agenda setting, analysis, policy creation, implementation and monitoring—within the 'citizens' participation areas', together with a long and apparently non-exhaustive list of different items that can hardly be reconciled to unity.

While this five-layer framework may be useful for characterization purposes, it leaves largely unattended the question, particularly relevant in a normative perspective of whether the 'e' addition has to be seen as a value itself, a by-product of the mechanization and computerization of Public Administration as a whole, or in which respects it actually improves the current performance of socio-political institutions (e.g. Rose et al.[11] and Sæbø et al.[12]). As Sæbø et al.[13] point out, 'the forms, structures and purposes of democratic participation are much discussed in the political sciences and political philosophy literatures. However these understandings are partially and inconsistently transferred to the eParticipation literature', which prevents an assessment of the organizational benefits and/or democratic gains related to ICT take-up for the redesign and restructuring of decision-making processes in the legislative, regulatory and policy domains.

To make progress in that direction, this paper assumes the viewpoint of the decision-makers themselves, particularly the regional ones. This derives from the evaluation of the IDEAL-EU project, which has leveraged on the managerial experience and expertise level on citizens' participation of three Regional Governments (Toscana in Italy, Poitou-Charentes in France and Catalunya in Spain). The project has been carried out in three main steps:

---

[7] Tambouris et al., 'A framework for scoping eParticipation', op. cit.

[8] Tambouris et al., 'A framework for assessing eParticipation projects and tools', op. cit.

[9] Anttiroiko, op. cit.

[10] Macintosh, op. cit.

[11] J. Rose, Å. Grönlund and K. V. Andersen, 'Introduction', in A. Avdic, K. Hedström, J. Rose and Å. Grönlund (eds), *Understanding eParticipation. Contemporary PhD eParticipation Research in Europe*, Örebro University Library, 2007. Available at: <http://www.demo-net.org> (accessed December 2009).

[12] Ø. Sæbø, J. Rose and L. S. Flak, 'The shape of eParticipation: characterizing an emerging research area', *Government Information Quarterly*, 25, 2008, pp. 400–428.

[13] Ibid.

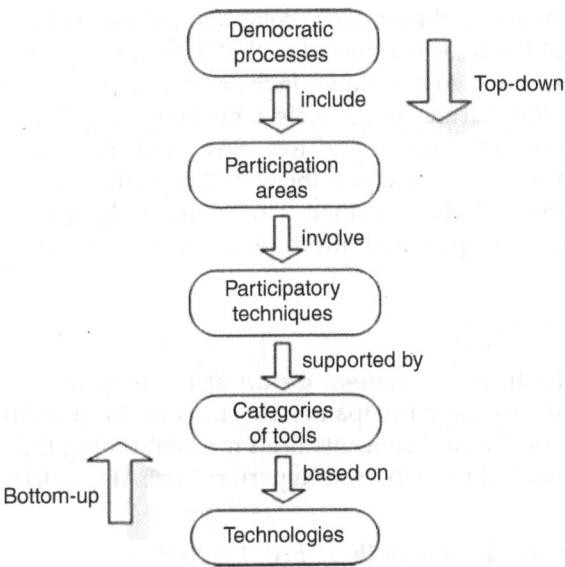

Figure 1. Five analytical layers for the scoping of eParticipation.
Source: E. Tambouris, N. Liotas, D. Kaliviotis and K. Tarabanis, 'A framework for scoping eParticipation', in *Proceedings of the 8th Annual International Digital Government Research Conference*, 2007.

(1) Deploying and disseminating in the three regions an innovative Social Networking Platform (SNP) that has allowed the distribution of thematic information and the realization of electronic debates, involving regional citizens and stakeholders, on the broad topic of climate change in Europe.

(2) Organizing on 15 November 2008 a Virtual Town Meeting (VTM), in the three regions simultaneously, in the venues of Firenze, Poitiers and Barcelona. The aim was to let regional young people discuss and vote on the most crucial issues at stake and on the related recommendations to European policy-makers, in particular to the Temporary Committee on Climate Change, to which the deliberation results were handed out.

(3) Laying the foundation of a European Network of Participatory Regions (http://www.demo-part.org), based on the successful track record of the three administrations involved in the project, and opened to other regional authorities active on (e)Participation experiences in Europe.

During the early project stages, an innovative participatory workflow model[14] and a corresponding technical architecture have been designed and trialled in the course of the pilots on climate change.[15] After performing the trials, the main characteristics of the initial workflow model have been revised and refined.

---

[14] A 'workflow model' is an established concept from management sciences. It is related to the study of the operational aspects of an activity of work: how are the tasks structured, how are they carried out, which is their correlative order, how are they synchronized, how flows the information that holds the tasks and how the fulfilment of the tasks is followed up (N. Russell, A. H. M. Hofstede, W. M. P. van der Aalst and N. Mulyar, *Workflow Control-Flow Patterns: A Revised View*, BPM Center Report, 2006).

[15] C. Colombo, M. Kunstelj, F. Molinari and L. Todorovski, 'Workflow modeling for participatory

The revision is based on the evidence collected and on the lessons learnt during the evaluation of the trials conducted in the three participating regions.

The paper is organized as follows. In the next section, we present the baseline conditions and the starting point for establishing the participatory workflow. The third section introduces the workflow and the supporting technical architecture. The fourth section puts the workflow in the context of prior work on practice and theory of eParticipation. Finally, the fifth section provides a brief summary and outlines potential directions for further research.

Baseline Conditions

This section introduces the state-of-the-art at the beginning of the IDEAL-EU project. It introduces the participatory practices in the three regions involved, establishes the background concepts used for establishing the workflow model and presents its initial version used to perform IDEAL-EU trials.

Former Participatory Practices in the IDEAL-EU Regions

The IDEAL-EU project has been performed by three European regions with long experience in citizen participation in public decision-making. This section describes the most important participatory practices in Catalonia, Regione Toscana and Poitou-Charentes, before the performance of the IDEAL-EU project trials.

Catalonia. In Catalonia, citizen participation in public decision-making has been introduced in the Catalan Government since 2004. The Directorate General (DG) for Citizen Participation was created with the aim of putting into practice the so-called 'New Governance' principles.

It is devoted to the promotion of citizen participation in the formulation and implementation of public policies of the Catalan Government. The DG for Citizen Participation promotes participatory experiences at local and regional level, gathering stakeholders and citizens to co-elaborate public policies at local and regional levels.

The DG for Citizen Participation also promotes the research and policy innovation in the field of democratic procedures analysing the ICT uses for democratic innovation. In this sense, it promoted the IDEAL-EU project, with the aim of launching a pilot experience of electronic citizen participation at the European level.

Regione Toscana. In Tuscany, citizen participation has been affirmed progressively as a mandatory requisite in planning socio-economic development in general. The rationale for an extension of concertation from collective bodies to citizens, relies on a mix of 'ideological' and 'pragmatic' considerations. The political will was to go beyond a 'plain vanilla' concertation with regional stakeholders and try new forms of political inclusion taking benefit from the long-standing 'cultural' tradition of civic engagement in Tuscany.

Footnote 15 continued
policy design: lessons from three European regions', in E. Tambouris and A. Macintosh (eds), *Proceedings of the ePART2009 Conference*, Trauner Verlag, Linz, 2009, pp. 101–111.

It looks for an increased scope for people's involvement in the key policy decisions that directly affect them.

The result of these efforts has been the first regional bill in Europe (Tuscany's Law No. 69 of 2007) dealing with the involvement of citizens in the legislative and policy design process. It has to be mentioned that prior to its drafting and approval by the Regional Council, the Cabinet started a collective discussion, which lasted almost two years and made use of both 'offline' and ICT tools, to identify the core issues and the possible guidelines of this legislative effort, committing to receive any kind of structured input from the numerous participatory experiences on course in the region.

Poitou-Charentes. In Poitou-Charentes, participatory democracy has been a constant since 2004. It has been gradually applied from the prior phase of the decisions to their evaluation afterwards. Since then, Participatory Forums bring together actors and citizens to co-elaborate the policies implemented by the region in all its fields of action.

It is worth mentioning that from 2005 on, the High Schools Participatory Budget is funded with an annual amount allocated of 10 million euros. It was a first in France and in the world (as the participatory budgets are mainly for municipalities and rarely applied to a regional level).

Since 2008, the first Participatory workshops and Citizens' Juries have been held to evaluate the regional public policies.

Summary and impact of the IDEAL-EU project. There is not a single way of promoting citizens' participation in public policies design. The experiences reported previously from the three regions clearly show the variety of approaches:

- In Catalonia, the Government has promoted and financially sustained participatory initiatives of its internal departments and participatory experiences of the Catalan local governments, with an increasing budget and reputation based on previous success stories.
- In Tuscany, the Administration has first established a model of 'cooperative governance' with its main stakeholders, then issued a specific law to discipline and regulate the participatory activities of lower level authorities (especially Municipalities) and civil society organizations.
- In Poitou-Charentes, the region is directly involved in organizing events, debates and other opportunities for public discussion, driven by their immediate goals and thematic orientation.

Now for the first time, thanks to the IDEAL-EU project, these three regions have been jointly experimenting with a same workflow of activities—combined with technical solutions such as the Social Networking Platform and the Virtual Town Meeting, and their related methodologies for moderated online discourses and deliberations. To explore what implications this unitary adoption and experimentation may induce in the respective decision-making processes, it is worth using the workflow model presented in the third section.

Participatory and Policy-Making Frameworks

As stated in the introduction, there are few models in the literature that characterize the eParticipation domain's basic elements and the relationships among them. Moreover, practically all of them are still in the development and refinement process (see Tambouris et al.,[16] Kalampokis et al.,[17] Aichholzer and Westholm,[18] and Bicking and Wimmer[19]). Moreover, none is specifically focused on representing and characterizing a participatory decision-making process within Public Administration. Therefore, in Colombo et al.,[20] we started to draft the IDEAL-EU workflow model from scratch, based on its desired characteristics.

There are two main features of our participatory workflow. On the one hand, it must support policy design and implementation, so it should follow the characteristics of the general policy-making process. On the other hand, it must have an informative and deliberative value for Public Administration, so it should have the characteristics of social or people-driven processes, where collaboration and ad hoc interaction are important as highly structured work steps. Based on these requirements, we employed three existing reference frameworks as starting points to develop the initial IDEAL-EU workflow model:

(a) Macintosh's representation of the policy-making (or more generally, public decision-making) process;[21]
(b) Freeman's stakeholders theory;[22] and
(c) Winograd and Flores' interaction model to formalize the actual collaboration among stakeholders.[23]

These will be shortly surveyed in the next three paragraphs.

Public decision-making process   To characterize the decision-making process of Public Administration we used a model that was first introduced by Anttiroiko[24] and then formalized by Macintosh.[25] It is composed of five high-level stages:

(1) *Agenda setting*: establishing the need for a policy or a modification of an existing one and defining what is the problem to be addressed.
(2) *Prior analysis*: defining the challenges and opportunities associated with the given agenda item, in order to produce a draft policy document (it can include: gathering evidence and knowledge from different sources; understanding the context, including the political context for the agenda item or developing a range of options).
(3) *Policy creation*: ensuring a good, workable policy document. Involves

---

[16] Tambouris et al., 'A framework for assessing eParticipation projects and tools', op. cit.; Tambouris et al., 'A framework for scoping eParticipation', op. cit.

[17] Kalampokis et al., op. cit.

[18] Aichholzer and Westholm, op. cit.

[19] Bicking and Wimmer, op. cit.

[20] Colombo et al., op. cit.

[21] Macintosh, op. cit.

[22] R. E. Freeman, *Strategic Management: A Stakeholder Approach*, Pittman, Boston, MA, 1984.

[23] T. Winograd and F. Flores, *Understanding Computers and Cognition: A New Foundation for Design*, Addison-Wesley Longman, Boston, MA, 1987.

[24] Anttiroiko, op. cit.

[25] Macintosh, op. cit.

a variety of mechanisms which can include: formal consultation, risk analysis, undertaking pilot studies and designing the implementation plan.
(4) *Policy implementation*: it can involve the development of legislation, regulation, guidance and a delivery plan.
(5) *Policy monitoring*: it involves the review of the policy in action, research evidence and views of users. Here there is the possibility to loop back to stage one.

Considering the basic characteristics of the IDEAL-EU workflow, we initially thought that it could cover only the first two and part of the third stage of the policy-making process, or be utilized only up to the level of proposal for future policy determination. However, after the project trials' execution, we realized that the final stages of the policy-making process (namely, implementation and monitoring) could be supported as well. Furthermore, as an original contribution emerged during the project assessment phase, it was decided to add a sixth stage (*Policy evaluation*), according to Ann Macintosh's model.[26]

This partly reflects the unexpected evolution that the project has taken with respect to initial provisions and anticipations. Basically, the formal date of the Town Meeting, which was originally set for spring 2009, had to be put forward to 15 November 2008 in order to ensure that the EP's Temporary Committee on Climate Change could include the results of this pan-European experiment in its final proceedings, scheduled for the end of November. As a result, the whole second year of the project has been dedicated to monitoring and self-assessment, and the Social Networking Platform (SNP) (www.ideal-debate.eu) has gained a prominent role in that respect.

First of all, the SNP was used in the first project months mainly to display and distribute thematic information on topics related to climate change. Starting in September 2008, it was used to hold online debates in preparation of the Virtual Town Meeting.

After the trials, the SNP continued to have new traffic after the conclusion of the IDEAL-EU trials, especially during the Copenhagen Conference on Climate Change. Furthermore, in 2009, it was further exploited by the Regional Administration of Tuscany in the context of 'Piazza Toscana', a participatory experience on the impact and benefits of the new law on participation. Finally, the Regional Network of Participatory Regions—officially launched in the last months of 2009 and being another permanent outcome of the IDEAL-EU project—uses the same platform for its own website (www.demo-part.org) to establish a permanent, multi-national community to promote eParticipation in Europe.

To sum up, the SNP showed its crucial importance for the IDEAL-EU workflow model implementation, in three different respects:

(a) Displaying and highlighting the most important subject matters and the key thematic issues at stake, as well as identifying the most appreciated debate axes by the SNP users, with a view to their possible replication in the VTM. This first aspect was particularly important in the Catalonia case. In this sense, it is worth mentioning the SNP feature allowing proposal prioritization through an e-voting mechanism.

---

[26] Macintosh, op. cit.

(b) Identifying the most active contributors, to be invited as participants in the VTM. This second aspect was particularly appreciated in the Poitou-Charentes case. The corresponding SNP features were the ranking of 'top contributors' and the possibility of contacting them, without violating their anonymity and privacy, by making use of the valid e-mail address they had provided upon registration.
(c) Monitoring the post-project participation and feedback, not only to the specific trial (which continued being disseminated throughout the second project year), but more generally, to the Regional Government's policies enhancing citizens' spaces of interactivity and discussion on any matters of public relevance. This third aspect better characterizes the Tuscany case and the main feature used is the flexibility of the SNP platform as a whole.

Description of involved actors and stakeholders. According to Freeman's stakeholder theory,[27] we identified six types of individuals, groups and organizations as key stakeholders of the IDEAL-EU workflow. They are presented in Table 1.

In general, stakeholders are defined as organizations, individuals or groups of individuals who have any kind of interest touched upon, contribute to or are affected by the IDEAL-EU workflow. From the descriptions of the tasks in Table 1, we can observe that some of them play a supporting role (like moderators and the technical staff), while others (like the regional decision-makers and the general public) are essential components of any participatory experiment, giving the rationale for its preparation, ensuring the quantity and quality of its results, and also showing its usefulness for the 'traditional' policy or law/regulation-making process.

Initial workflow model. Another point of reference for drafting the IDEAL-EU workflow model was a known business process modelling technique named action workflow,[28] which relies on the interaction model introduced by Winograd and Flores.[29] The latter is based on an understanding of how knowledge workers interact and collaborate. Hence, its strength lies in the ability of modelling social processes (i.e. people-driven processes)—exactly what we needed to design the IDEAL-EU workflow.

Action workflow captures and coordinates the ways people with different skills and knowledge collaborate on business decisions. Collaboration depends on one individual or group (the 'customers') requesting some specific job from another individual or group (the 'performers'). The two parties negotiate an agreement in which the performers commit to do the job, complete it and the customers assess the job to see that it meets the negotiated agreement.

This collaboration process can be depicted as a closed-loop interaction model and presents the atomic unit of work. A business process then becomes a series of loops, one main loop and several sub-process loops, representing interactions

---

[27] Freeman, op. cit.
[28] ActionWorks, 'ActionWorks, the Action Technologies business process analysis and redesign methodology, and the Business Interaction Model', Action Technologies Inc., 2008, available at: <http://www.actiontech.com> (accessed 5 June 2008).
[29] Winograd and Flores, op. cit.

Table 1. Stakeholders of the IDEAL-EU workflow

Stakeholder	Description	Major tasks
Owners	Representatives of the regional administration, including elected officials and strategic advisors	Political management and support of the participatory workflow model
Decision-makers[a]	EU Parliament members, more specifically the members of the Temporary Committee on Climate Change of the EU Parliament	Integration of the participative workflow in the decision-making proceedings
Practitioners	Competent[b] civil servants staff and climate change and/or participatory methodologies' experts	Agenda setting, preparing materials in support of the debate, collecting the results and synthesizing the conclusions
Moderators	Moderators and facilitators of the public debates, invited by the owners, also including voluntary people and domain experts as above	Moderation of debates and deliberations collection, including resolution of the non-technical problems that could arise during workflow execution
Participants[c]	Interested citizens, businesses, civil society organizations, NGOs, political groups: randomly selected, purposefully invited or self-invited (e.g. SNP subscribers)	Active participation in the debates and deliberations, including provision of opinions, comments, ideas and proposals
Technical support group	Information Technology experts (regional staff)	Resolution of the technical problems that may arise during workflow execution

[a] Individuals, groups or organizations that are affected by the workflow results. They can either be 'internal' or 'external' to the public administration 'owning' the debates.
[b] The notion of competence here is used in its legal meaning.
[c] Users of the Social Network Platform and participants in the Virtual Town Meetings.

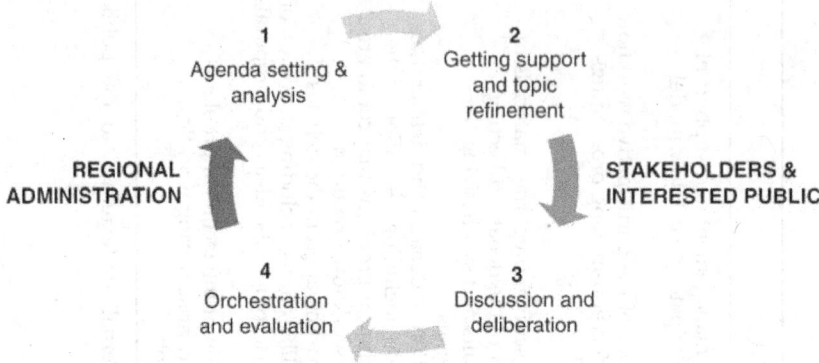

Figure 2. Initial eParticipation workflow model.

and commitments taking place among collaborating people involved at different stages of the overall process.

Following the idea of a business interaction model defined by action workflow combined with the extended (six-stage) general policy-making process model, we drafted an initial version of the IDEAL-EU workflow, depicted in Figure 2. It includes all the required activities for the execution of IDEAL-EU project trials.

While a complete description of the four phases and related activities are available in Colombo et al.,[30] we provide a summary here:

- The first stage '*Agenda setting and analysis*' is of high strategic importance, since it determines the key objectives and topics of the participatory experiment and how to establish and/or strengthen the enabling conditions for a successful experience in the envisaged community. It includes activities related to identification of the policy-making issue and deliberation of the information to potential participants through the use of the multilingual SNP.
- The second stage '*Getting support and topic refinement*' is aimed at raising the awareness of stakeholders and the general public about the objectives and contents of planned discussions and deliberations, as well as convincing them of the importance of the particular participatory experience approached. It includes activities related to raising awareness of the relevant policy-makers and potential participants through dissemination.
- The third stage '*Discussion and deliberation*' refers to the two supporting loops of the eParticipation workflow, that is, the discussion within the SNP and the VTM. Its objective is to enable an informed discussion and deliberation on concrete and relevant legislative or policy-making issues, which will become inputs for further deliberations or legislative/administrative determinations by the 'appointed' decision-makers. This stage includes two kinds of participatory processes of virtual moderated debates on the SNP and simultaneous small-group discussions and polls during the VTM. The aim of the SNP debates is to create critical mass conditions for the start-up of the following stage of proper deliberation to be held in the VTM. There, participants carry on simultaneous discussions in small groups, individually

---

[30] Colombo et al., op. cit.

Table 2. Decomposition of the IDEAL-EU workflow

Public decision-making process	IDEAL-EU workflow modules	Collaborating stakeholders	IDEAL-EU technical components
1. Agenda Setting	Agenda setting and analysis	• Decision-makers • Owners • Practitioners	None (offline activity)
2. Prior Analysis	Getting support and topic refinement	• Practitioners • Participants • Moderators	SNP
3. Policy Creation	Discussion and deliberation	• Participants • Moderators	VTM
4. Policy Implementation		• Decision-makers	
5. Policy Monitoring	Orchestration and evaluation: evaluation	• Participants • Moderators • Owners	SNP
6. Policy Evaluation			None (offline activity)
=	Orchestration and evaluation: orchestration	• Decision-makers • Practitioners • Moderators • Technical support group	SNP VTM

expressing their opinions through an electronic polling system. The main aim is to generate structured deliberations and meaningful summaries of the various positions that emerged during the debate, so as to produce clear inputs for the 'traditional' decision-making actors and processes within or outside the regional administration involved.

- The fourth stage *'Orchestration and evaluation'* is aimed at supervising, monitoring and assessing the results of a smooth and effective performance of the workflow activities, both under a technical and a non-technical perspective, throughout the whole duration of the project. It includes activities related to resolution of problems that may arise during execution of the workflow as well as evaluation and assessment of the execution. Its main aim is to prepare and submit the results of the participatory efforts to the relevant policy-makers.

Table 2 presents the relationship between the four activity modules of the initial IDEAL-EU workflow and the six stages of the public decision-making process introduced by earlier research on eParticipation. Stakeholders' roles and tasks are matched with the more appropriate components of the cycle, according to the collaborative nature of the IDEAL-EU workflow modules. The last column specifies the technical platforms (if any) used to support the respective activities.

In our initial view, the IDEAL-EU workflow should end at the policy creation stage, since it was mainly intended to define and prioritize (by means of the SNP and particularly VTM debates) the key issues at stake, including the formulation of guidelines for policy-makers—in this case, the EP Temporary Committee of Climate Change. Hence, its outputs were expected to represent just the input for future developments in the legislative, regulatory and/or governmental action environments (i.e. what is called policy implementation). However, due to the special and partly unexpected course taken by the project activities, the IDEAL-EU Consortium had the opportunity to appreciate the SNP role at two different stages of public decision-making:

- Firstly, as a complement to agenda setting and particularly support to topic refinement.
- Secondly, as an additional tool for policy monitoring and evaluation.[31]

The Final Workflow Model and Technical Architecture

This section provides a description of the consolidated achievements of the IDEAL-EU project. Before introducing the final workflow model in the second subsection, we will present the technical components of the supporting architecture.

Technical Components

Jointly with the previous efforts, we also drafted a technical architecture, which aimed to visualize the technological components supporting the IDEAL-EU workflow model implementation and the way they were linked to the various activities (mainly showing the data flows between them). The technical architecture also specifies how the stakeholders of the IDEAL-EU workflow interact with the specific technological components.

As should be evident from the previous description, the underlying technical platform is an integral part of the IDEAL-EU workflow model. The two basic technological components through which the workflow was implemented are:

- The Social Networking Platform (SNP), allowing tailored information to be published and moderated online debates be performed on the selected issue.
- The Virtual Town Meeting (VTM) infrastructure, enabling users to take part in deliberative sessions and to formulate proposals for future policy or legislation-making in a structured and controlled way.

The IDEAL-EU Social Networking Platform (http://www.ideal-debate.eu) has been developed in Web 2.0 technology and has been made available in four languages: English, Italian, Catalan and French.

A Town Meeting is a form of structured participation in local government where the community is invited by government officials to formulate suggestions or provide feedback on specific policy issues. In its modern version—the Virtual Town Meeting (VTM)—a dedicated web application makes it possible to support a similar interaction structure among hundreds of participants located in different venues in real time.

---

[31] Strictly speaking, some regional activities with the SNP can be seen as out of the scope of the original instance of the IDEAL-EU workflow, since their objectives are different. But they nonetheless position themselves at later stages of the public decision-making process than policy creation, which we take as evidence of a wider potential of the IDEAL-EU workflow model than initially expected.

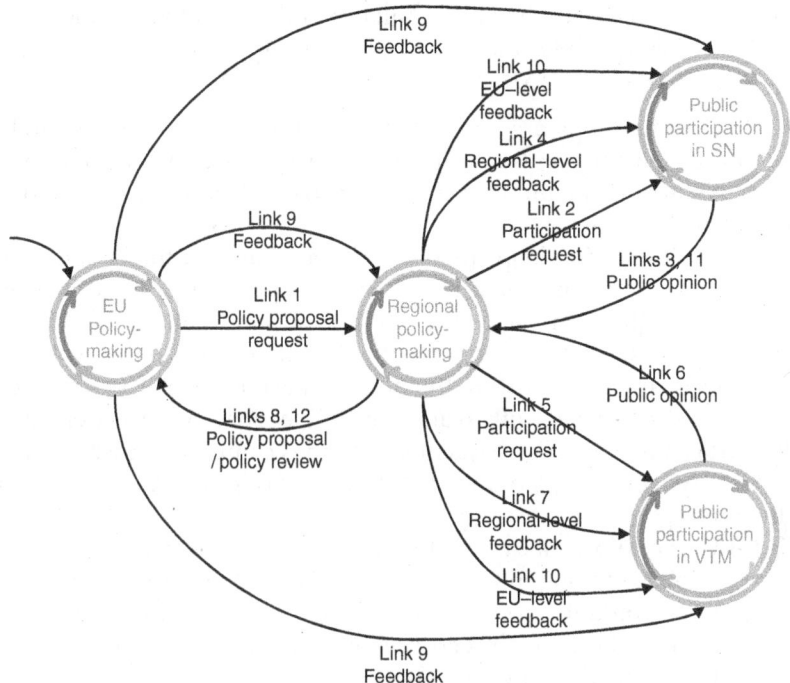

Figure 3. Participatory workflow model—'the IDEAL-EU tulip'.

The IDEAL-EU 'Tulip'

When drafting the IDEAL-EU workflow model, we started from the assumption that this represents only the main interaction loop and the basic stages of the participatory workflow, establishing a framework for further development (see Figure 2). In particular there was a need to have a more detailed demonstration of the activities and actors taking part in the workflow, having in mind especially:

- Better representation of the three levels of policy-making involved in the IDEAL-EU project (the EU, the regional and the local level).
- Better representation of the activities supported by two technological components involved in the workflow (SNP and VTM).
- Better visibility of the interconnections and influences between all of the above.

Thus, the initial interaction loop was multiplied into four interconnected loops as depicted in Figure 3, representing four instantiations of the public decision-making cycle on three decision-making levels:

- Decision-making at EU level (in the IDEAL-EU case: the European Parliament elaborating the new policy agenda on Climate Change and Sustainable Energy).
- Decision-making at regional level resulting in policy proposals for the EU level, or invoked by the latter to activate a participatory experiment with the population.
- Decision-making at operational level ensuring citizens' participation in the EU or regional policy-making, legislative or regulatory process and being

associated to the usage of the new familiar methods and tools deployed in the IDEAL-EU trials, namely, the Social Networking Platform (SNP) and the Virtual Town Meeting (VTM).

The four interaction loops are connected to each other in order to emphasize the main inputs/outputs and data flows between the various actors involved. The connection arrows are numbered in order to emphasize the normal order of activities in the workflow.

Each of four interaction loops involves all four stages of the initial workflow model (Agenda setting and analysis, Getting support and topic refinement, Discussion and deliberation, and Orchestration and evaluation) although using different approaches/platforms and oriented to different audiences. This ensures that the request for action from the upper level is properly handled and completed by the lower one, with evaluation and feedback information provided to all the parties involved. Consequently, activities comprising each stage of the initial workflow were adapted and distributed among the interaction loops to which they refer.

IDEAL-EU workflow starts at the EU level, by starting a legislative, regulatory or policy-making initiative in a certain problem area. At this stage a working group, a committee or other association of political representatives at EU level recognizes the problem and sets an initial agenda for discussion and deliberation (1st stage of the EU level loop).

While the EU level can autonomously undertake a consultation campaign or other forms of direct involvement of citizens in the decision-making process, using the facilities that are independently available to it (such as the 'Your Voice in Europe' portal[32] and the 'Interactive Policy Making' tool[33]), the big value of the IDEAL-EU workflow model comes from leveraging the regional dimension in particular.

Thus, after raising awareness and getting support from the relevant EU level stakeholders (2nd stage of the EU level loop), a formal request is submitted to the regional level (link #1) to activate a participatory experiment.

At the regional level, the owners of the initiative further develop the received agenda by a detailed analysis of the topic introduced and the preparation of a joint experiment with Social Networks and Virtual Town Meetings (1st stage of the regional level loop). Regional representatives can raise the awareness of stakeholders and of the general public using different communication methods. They also motivate them to attending the planned events (2nd stage of the regional level loop).

Electronic Participation is then realized in two ways. First, Social Networking is performed in preparation of the Town Meeting and as a motivation means for public participation (links #2, #3 and #4).[34] Second, Virtual Town Meetings are carried out, aimed at structuring the public opinion relevant to the issue at hand (links #5, #6 and #7). During each exercise, the agenda defined by the requester of the participatory exercise is further detailed and adjusted to specific objectives,

---

[32] < http://ec.europa.eu/yourvoice/ >.

[33] < http://ec.europa.eu/yourvoice/ipm/index_en.htm >.

[34] Actually, as shown in the previous section *Public decision-making process*, the SNP role has become prominent in the IDEAL-EU project, also for monitoring purposes and as an independent platform for issue discussion and prioritization.

circumstances and audiences (1st stage of the SNP and VTM loops), specific actions are taken to present the exercise to the audiences as well as to motivate them for participation (2nd stage of the SNP and VTM loops), discussion and deliberation activities using SNP and VTM are carried out (3rd stage of the SNP and VTM loops), and finally results are evaluated and the resulting public opinion is submitted to the regional policy-makers (4th stage of the SNP and VTM loops).

After holding both of these participatory exercises, the owners of the initiative discuss the inputs received (3rd stage of the regional level loop), evaluate the results and prepare policy proposals for the EU level (4th stage of the regional level loop and link #8). Discussions and evaluations then repeat themselves at the EU level (3rd and 4th stage of EU level loop). Finally, the workflow is completed by the provision of feedback information to the relevant regional level policy-makers (link #9) and to the general public (links #9 and #10).

Some activities are then repeated in the form of monitoring, evaluation and consideration of post-project participation, as outlined in Table 2 (links #11 and #12).

Discussion

This section seeks to gather and analyse the main lessons learned from the implementation of the workflow within the IDEAL-EU project. In continuation, it highlights the potential benefits of the workflow for practitioners, governments and researchers of eParticipation.

Lessons Learnt from the IDEAL-EU Trials

The IDEAL-EU eParticipation trials performed in each of the regions followed the outlined eParticipation workflow. Thus, the trials involved discussions and deliberations with the goal of contributing to shape a common EU agenda on climate change issues, by allowing young citizens to participate in public policy design. This section presents the main lessons learned from the project implementation in the three regions.

(1) *Participation cannot be improvised.* Participation is fragile, delicate and sensitive. It requires careful planning and professional, high-quality execution. eParticipation adds potential and instruments that can make room for a structured integration of digital resources into public decision-making. However, it can only have a future if we do it well, show its results and demonstrate its usefulness. Otherwise, not only do we risk that participation will not solve the problems laid down before it, but even that they can be worsened by it.

Thus, in the stage of agenda setting and analysis, it is important to keep in mind a clear reference framework for the participatory activities. It is necessary to establish the debate's limits and rules and the main subjects and issues to be discussed, making clear those that are not under discussion. This approach can support trust building around this type of initiative and also avoid creating false expectations with the corresponding frustrations. In the

Tuscany experience, the establishment of a permanent forum of discussion with and within the citizenry, based on Social Networking principles, is a concrete step towards a more mature approach to 'top-down' participation.

(2) *Two-way feedback is essential to make participation credible.* In a representative democracy, the final decisions belong to the Government, which is held responsible for its actions through the electoral cycle. But in the new governance framework,[35] decision-makers can take into better account the contribution of the citizens in the elaboration of some public policies. Thus, two-way feedback (not only from, but also to citizens) is essential to a good participation, in two respects: first, by clarifying from the beginning that only some or a few citizens' contributions received will be taken onboard, depending on their usefulness. Second, by describing the actual impact that the specific participatory trial has had on the final decision taken: what has been called 'return' in the Catalan experience, or 'evaluation' in Figure 2. Here again, digitalization of Government–citizens interaction and the take-up of process level innovation as described in this paper seems crucial to differentiate participation from mere opinion polls and ensure global accountability to the citizenry. The success of this strategy, halfway between two falsely conflicting models, direct and representative democracy, allows us to move towards what constitutes our point of reference: deliberative democracy.[36]

(3) *Relationships are crucial: the importance of getting support.* Citizen participation experiments mostly deal with public sector's transformation and decentralization. In Government cultures with deeply rooted tradition of specialization and fragmentation, any project that transcends boundaries is very difficult to bring to fruition. Thus, it is very important to work in cooperation with other internal departments or external authorities, which brings us face to face with one of the most serious challenges of the current Public Administration: the need for capacity building of the civil servants involved. In this context, there are two additional difficulties to deal with: the possible distrust on participation from people without special knowledge on the issues to be discussed, and the political leaders' fear of the consequences of participation in terms of diminution of their influential power over citizens. To manage also these difficulties, civil officials have to work towards building trust by showing results, respect and the flexibility to adapt to each case.

(4) Administrations can change. It is important to foster a participatory culture within the Government and also within participants themselves. The difficulties here are enormous because they involve clashing with age-old inertias. However, it is important to rediscover some concepts that others have tried to banish from Public Administration: patience, conviction and trustworthiness. A participatory culture helps avoid tensions, conflicts and the tendency of individuals to attempt to dominate the proceedings of

---

[35] R. A. W. Rhodes, 'The new governance: governing without government', *Political Studies*, 44, 1996, pp. 652–667.

[36] B. Ackerman and J. S. Fishkin, *Deliberation Day*, Yale University Press, New Haven, CT, 2004; J. Fishkin, *The Voice of the People. Public Opinion and Democracy*, Yale University Press, New Haven, CT, 1995.

participatory processes. On the other hand, it gives incentives for participants to adhere to basic rules of mutual respect, listening to each other, and will to cooperate and reach agreements. A good management of participation also requires to soothe these tensions and to generate learning processes amongst all participating parties. As a result, efforts should be focused as much on the short as the long term, aiming to establish the basis for an active, politically engaged, citizenry.

(5) *A good communication strategy is essential*—especially when dealing with a policy that aims to call on individual citizen behaviour, like in the fight to reduce carbon footprints—and more generally because in these days a policy's visibility depends to large extent on the amount of coverage it receives from the media.

Benefits for Practitioners

The IDEAL-EU trials experience has been very useful to test the initially designed workflow and has allowed the participant regions to open up ad hoc participation spaces, where Internet users and particularly young citizens have had the opportunity to be part of a decision-making process, being endowed with enough information to express their informed judgement and to vote for specific and timely proposals to be included in the European policy-making agenda.

Overall, the project has been successful in integrating into a single process model what were identified at the time of the proposal preparation (August 2007) as the three main drivers of eParticipation, namely:

- Access, that is, the empowerment of an increasing number of citizens (particularly those belonging to specific age groups or social classes) to overcome existing gaps in infrastructure, equipment and training that prevent them from fully participating in the Internet's 'communitarian life'. In that respect, the IDEAL-EU consortium chose to focus its trial activities on young people as a single target group in the three regional communities alike. Looking at this with a critical view, the problem of access, which is very age dependent, may have been somehow avoided in this way, particularly with respect to the Social Networking Platform.
- Awareness, that is, the customization of eGovernment/eParticipation resources to make and keep citizens updated about the true dimension of the issues at stake, ultimately allowing an informed judgement—not just the expression of a 'wish' rather than a 'will', or even worse, a contradictory if ever binding statement. In particular, the IDEAL-EU consortium decided to leverage the recent rise of the so-called Web 2.0, where active citizens in social networking experience innovative ways and new opportunities to improve their knowledge on matters of public relevance. In that respect, the recommendation to carry on with the SNP maintenance after the project's end seems particularly apt to ensuring a growing level of awareness in the population, as a precondition for new and successful workflow instantiations.
- Debate, that is, the use of innovative methods and tools to let people discuss, interact and 'have their say', in such a way that 'the people's will' could be objectivized, documented, measured and prioritized, and that the new ideas,

hints, contributions emerging from this 'grassroots democracy' could actually reach policy-makers and provide benefits to the public decision-making process. Again using a critical view, it has been shown by the project results that moderation is crucial to reach an effective aggregation of citizens' preferences, and that the distribution of feedback information is as important as the one of prior information, particularly to ensure replication over time.

Preliminary cost–benefit analysis performed within the IDEAL-EU project did not come to a safe conclusion in terms of actual savings of time and effort for the regional civil servants using the workflow. Some reasons for this are the need to make recourse to external moderators and facilitators for the debates, and the high cost of setting up a Virtual Town Meeting infrastructure from scratch. Nonetheless, it is worth mentioning that far higher costs and efforts might be needed in order to achieve the same results with non-electronic participation methods and the political advantages of civic involvement in terms of trust, consensus building and electoral turnout.

Taken together, the IDEAL-EU workflow, its documented instances and the cost–benefit analysis associated to it may represent a significant progress—not only conceptual, but also operational—towards the introduction of more stable ways of integrating the 'citizens' will' into democratic decision-making at the regional level in Europe.

The IDEAL-EU technical infrastructure provides a customizable Open Source Software platform for creating and maintaining an ICT-enabled participation environment for regional citizens and stakeholders, capable of supporting a wide range of public decision-making processes, including those launched by third parties. Such an eParticipation environment, supported by the IDEAL-EU workflow model, can seamlessly integrate into any of the standard process stages of legislation, regulation and Government action in general. Thanks to the IDEAL-EU manuals, a collection of guidelines will enable public officials to carry out their process-related tasks and policy-makers to keep full control of the ongoing discussions and deliberations. These are in our opinion, among the most important requirements to ensure a fair level of sustainability of any technology and methodology for eParticipation.

Contributions to the eParticipation Discipline

The scientific value of the IDEAL-EU workflow model can be easily appreciated in the three following respects.

First of all, it comes as a result of an iterative construction process. As Krimmer[37] pointed out, there are two basic approaches known in IS research for the creation of process models:

(a) the deductive approach, starting from a theoretical construction and then adapting it to reality, based on problems in implementation,

---

[37] R. Krimmer, 'Case study-based development of an eParticipation process model', in A. Avdic, K. Hedström, J. Rose and Å. Grönlund (eds), *Understanding eParticipation. Contemporary PhD eParticipation Research in Europe*, Örebro University Library, 2007, available at: <http://www.demo-net.org> (accessed December 2009).

(b) or the inductive approach, starting from the current experiences and an analysis thereof, on which to build a best-of model.

In the IDEAL-EU project, we have used a combination of the two approaches; namely, we have provided an initial draft of the workflow model and then used it as a guideline for concrete implementation. Following the evaluation of the regional trials executed, we have provided a final and extended version of the workflow, covering a wide range of public decision-making environments. It has been demonstrated during the project that this has the potential of seamlessly and permanently integrating into the pre-existing socio-cultural, juridical and political set-up of the participant regions.

Secondly, the model comes explicitly as an integration of the public decision-making process, whenever participation from citizens and other stakeholders is required. Again, two basic perspectives exist in the literature, as far as the vision and description of public decision-making is concerned:

(a) The rational choice theory, according to which all viable alternatives are first listed, then weighed against each other, together with the costs of attaining them, and the final decision is the one that maximizes the net present value over time. This has evolved into the bounded rationality theory,[38] criticizing the former with the argument that being information limited or costly and decision-makers lacking the time and skills to consider all the alternatives available, they restrict themselves to picking up 'the most satisfactory' (rather than 'the optimal') option known.

(b) A set of managerial and organizational theories, taking into account the complexity and unpredictability of decision-making in conditions of uncertainty and under the pressure of diverse stakeholders,[39] possibly resulting in adaptive behaviour,[40] imitation effects,[41] 'solutions in search of problems',[42] irrational choices 'resold' externally as rational,[43] etc.

Both perspectives, in our opinion, ignore the importance of analysing Public Administration processes as framing civil servants' and elected representatives' behaviour and potentially being a vehicle and driver of change and innovation.

According to Georgakopoulos et al.,[44] the 'common-sense' definition of administrative process in any organization—as distinct from production and sales—involves repetitive, predictable activities with simple task coordination rules and that rely on humans for most of the decisions and work performed.

---

[38] H. A. Simon, *Models of Man: Social and Rational. Mathematical Essays on Rational Human Behavior in a Social Setting*, John Wiley, New York, 1957; and J. G. March, 'Bounded rationality, ambiguity and the engineering of choice', *The Bell Journal of Economics*, 9(2), 1978, pp. 587–608.

[39] Freeman, op. cit.

[40] C. E. Lindblom, 'The science of "muddling through"', *Public Administration Review*, 19(2), 1959, pp. 79–88.

[41] P. J. DiMaggio and W. W. Powell, 'The iron cage revisited. Institutional isomorphism and collective rationality in organisational fields', *American Sociological Review*, April 1983, pp. 147–160.

[42] M. D. Cohen, J. G. March and J. P. Olsen, 'A garbage can model of organizational choice', *Administrative Science Quarterly*, 17, 1972, pp. 1–25.

[43] D. Stone, *Policy Paradox, the Art of Political Decision Making*, W. W. Norton, New York, 2001.

[44] D. Georgakopoulos, M. Hornick and A. Sheth, 'An overview of workflow management: from process modeling to workflow automation infrastructure', *Distributed and Parallel Databases*, 3, 1995, pp. 119–153.

Table 3. Future instantiations of the IDEAL-EU workflow

Analytical layers	IDEAL-EU workflow model		
Democratic processes	Policy-making	Law-making	Regulation
Participation areas	Climate change and energy???	???	???
Participatory techniques	Social Networking and Town Meeting methodology		
Category of tools	SNP and VTM		
Based on technologies	Drupal, PHP, MySql...		

However, what can be seen as a trivial or routine activity in a private business becomes the ordinary way of proceeding in the public sector. This is clearly the case of the legislative process, for instance, which is bound by predefined, known and hardly modifiable rules, otherwise depending on the aggregation of human preferences (i.e. the votes of elected members of parliament), as far as its final outcomes are concerned.

Rules, rather than discretion, is the environment where we would like to see our workflow model transplanted and rooted, believing that it could ease the task of both decision-makers and consulted citizens and stakeholders, leading to better laws, regulations and policies. Experiences like the one of the Tuscany Region, first in Europe to pass a specific bill on public participation, are worth exploring and monitoring closely in that respect.

Finally, there is a need for a more systematic approach to the classification of Public Administration processes where the integration of eParticipation is not only viable, but also politically and pragmatically fruitful.

Evolving from Tambouris *et al.*'s[45] framework, which was also depicted in Figure 1 in the introduction, we can conceptually map the IDEAL-EU workflow as depicted in Table 3. The goal of the IDEAL-EU project was to deploy and validate a participatory policy-making process on the issue of climate change in Europe. In this table, the question marks highlight additional deployment opportunities for the IDEAL-EU workflow model, which imply a number of theoretical as well as empirical challenges to become 'embedded' in the legal, political and social contexts of European Public Administration.

Conclusion

The IDEAL-EU project has been a good experience in terms of involving citizens in political participation, decision-making processes and deliberative procedures. IDEAL-EU has been an opportunity to test and develop a pilot experience related with ICT use in citizen participation experiences. The main achievements in this sense have been testing an Internet-based electronic debate (through the Social Networking Platform implementation and use), and testing electronic tools usage for citizen participation sessions to be held offline (through the Virtual Town Meeting).

---

[45] Tambouris *et al.*, 'A framework for scoping eParticipation', op. cit.

This experience has brought us some interesting ideas that are worth mentioning here. An electronic debate platform could be used for maintaining previous debates online, detect the main opinions, standpoints and arguments among participants and publicizing documents of interest for the participatory process. ICTs could also be used in offline participatory meetings mainly in the connection of the several offline sessions held in different parts of the territory.

ICTs have a big potential for citizen participation in public decision-making, although their performance and relevance in participatory processes is highly related to the design and implementation of the project and the political will. In this sense, ICT tools have to be at the participatory process service, not the other way round. In order to allow the discussion and deliberation workflow stage, it is very important to ensure a deliberative process takes place during offline sessions, allowing participants enough time to debate. It is also important to facilitate the virtual debates and take care to maintain electronically the coherence within the process; finally, it is decisive to sustain coherence between the offline process and the virtual debates.

ICTs have many potentialities for improving political processes and participatory experiences. In this sense, ICTs provide easy and direct access to information, allowing transparency of the government management. ICTs also facilitate a multilevel communication without time or space limits. However there are some challenges in relation to participatory experiences. Firstly, the digital divide entails inequalities among people, regions and institutions connected to the digital world and the disconnected ones. It also establishes inequalities among connected people, regarding the quality of the access and the use of e-tools.

Incorporation of ICTs into participatory experiences maintaining also the offline deliberation, allows us to take advantage of the potentialities of ICTs—mainly at informative and communicative level, avoiding their main challenges, maintaining the potentialities of offline experiences—such as socialization values and the creation of a participatory culture.

Among the key implications of the IDEAL-EU workflow model is that for a successful integration of eParticipation in the public decision-making process, it will be useful to adopt the process vision as a guideline for both institutional change and operational implementation of innovation. In our view, the scope and potential of eParticipation for reforming and modernizing Public Administration is much larger than simply responding to political disengagement with a supplement of transparency and accountability from the Government's side, and has only to a small extent been exploited so far.

Therefore, the framework of eParticipation should be extended, including to a much larger extent process analysis and (re)engineering. In this respect, existing modelling and evaluation paradigms (such as the Workflow Management Systems and the CAF, Common Assessment Framework, in the domain of quality management) could prove to be useful for the development and establishment of new behavioural and procedural rules that may become the building blocks of a more participatory Government (or Governance) in the years to come.

Of course, an ICT infrastructure (better if Open Source) and a set of methods and tools like the ones developed in our project are also important for a long run implementation of eParticipation, which brings about new requirements in terms of cultural adaptation of the civil servants and political staff, well ahead of their professional training. But we are convinced that almost all that is needed from a technical viewpoint is already here, while the most critical challenge is how to move forward from these 'one-shot' and 'ad hoc' trials, particularly towards the permanent coverage of mission critical functions of Public Administration. Some ideas that we would like to highlight are the following:

- The 'collective wisdom' ensures the provision of more and better ideas that nobody on their own could ever imagine. In that respect, public decision-making has always much more to gain than to lose in terms of quality, efficiency, timeliness, from a structured recourse to citizens' involvement and participation.
- The alternance of 'online' (= debate) and 'offline' (= awareness raising) moments remains critical in any participatory process. People are not easily engaged at all, it's up to Governments to make (even more than just) the first move towards them.
- eParticipation should not undermine 'offline' participation. It is very important to maintain the coherence and a fluid information exchange between offline and electronic debates.
- The same applies when different electronic tools are employed, such as the SNP and VTM.
- ICTs should be at the citizen's participation service, not the other way round.
- Finally, it is very important to endow electronic debates of the same participatory guarantees than the offline ones.

Acknowledgements

This research was made possible in part by a co-funding of the European Commission to the IDEAL-EU project, a Preparatory Action in the area of eParticipation, and by a close collaboration with the Special Committee on Climate Change at the European Parliament, chaired by former MEP Guido Sacconi. However, the opinions expressed in this paper are solely of the authors and do not involve any of the EU institutions. We acknowledge the work of all the IDEAL-EU team and thank them for their comments and those provided by the anonymous reviewers.

Clelia Colombo is a Researcher at the Autonomous University of Barcelona and an eDemocracy and eParticipation officer at the General Directorate for Citizen Participation of the Catalan Government. Clelia has a PhD in Political Science.

Mateja Kunstelj is Senior Lecturer and Researcher at the University of Ljubljana, Faculty of Administration.

Francesco Molinari is a Researcher at the University of Siena, Dipartimento Studi Aziendali e Sociali.

Ljupco Todorovski is Assistant Professor, scientific collaborator and researcher at the University of Ljubljana, Faculty of Administration.

Index

Page numbers in **Bold** represent Figures
Page numbers in *Italics* represent Tables

accountability 14
advanced information technologies 13–35; Greek parliament and LEX-IS project 13–35, *see also* LEX-IS project
Aichholzer, G.; and Westholm, H. 117
Ajzen, I.; and Fishbein, M. 41
Albania 8–9, 38
Albanian Telegraphic Agency (ATA) 38, 48
Anttiroiko, A. 122; *et al* 117–18
argument nodes 19
assemblage characteristics 63–4; adaption and repair 64; conversion, linking and plumbing 64; episodes and interventions 64; installed base 64; redesign and administrative routines 64
assemblages and sense-making 59–76; e-participation tool construction and implementation 59–76; features 63–4; Partecipa.Net system 61–5, *see also* ontology; sense-making
axiomatic relations 111, *see also* ontology

Barber, B. 1
Bench-Capon, T.; and Visser, P. 112
Bicking, M.; and Wimmer, M. 117
BLOG 99–114; purposes and representation 108–9
bottom up planning process 10, 118–19; approach 109; enhancement 113

Census Bureau (US) 100
Charalabidis, Y.; Loukis, E. and Macintosh, A. 1–11
Ciborra, C. 65–6
collaboration 98–9
Colombo, C.; *et al* 10, 117–38
Common Assessment Framework (CAF) 137
compendium tool 19
competitive capitalism 8
Conroy, M.; and Evans-Crowley, J. 104
consensus logic 114
Content Management System (CMS) 62

Contracts of Voluntary Cohabitation 18, 26, 29–30; e-consultation documents 18–19; fourth article visualization **20**; justification report visualization 18, **20**; main article titles 33
cooperative governance 121
Copenhagen Conference on Climate Change 123
Council of Europe 77
cyber cafés 74

Davis, F.; *et al* 41
Debian GNU/Linux operating system 106
Delphi 65
democratic processes 118; five layer framework 118–19, 122–3
Demos software application 61–4
digital divide 6
Digital Strategy (2006–2013) document 83
Dilemmas in a General Theory of Planning (Rittel and Weber) 15

e-consultations 5, 18–19, 89; agenda-setting/decision-making/policy forming 3, *see also* LEX-IS project
e-decision-making 77
e-Democracy 77; deficits 3, 37; systems 40–1
e-dialogos (Spain) 90–1
e-forums 18–19, 80, 89; installations (Western Balkans) **39**; structured 21–31; usefulness and ease of use 24–6, **24–5**, *see also* LEX-IS Project
e-Government 59; Action Plan (EU) 77; readiness 93
e-petition spaces 6
e-petition system 90
e-polls 39, 62, 80, 87–92
e-survey 90–1
e-tools 97–115; discussion and polling 39; Web 2.0 for PIT 104–9
electronic participation pilot studies 37–58; evaluation results 44–51; future research 51–2; mechanisms 39; operational model

INDEX

39–40, **40**; regional and local level authorities in Greece and Spain 77–96; research 65–7; systems evaluation methodology 40–4; Western Balkans National News Agency 38–40, *see also* Political Evaluation Questionnaire; Technology Acceptance Model

elitist model 3

Encyclopaedia Britannica 100

eParticipation initiatives 77–96; categorization 118–19; frameworks and criteria 78–9, *see also* regional and local level authorities

eParticipation systems evaluation methodology 40–4; attitudes 51; conclusions 51–2; model 40–4, **40**; questionnaire design 42–3; research hypotheses 43–4; steps followed 42; success factors **41**, *see also* TAM

European Commission 14; Sixth Framework Programme 38

European Network of Participatory Regions 119

European Union 9, 97; Consortium 128; e-Government strategic aims 90, 94; and e-participation research project funding 77; FP5 and Preparatory Action programmes 77; IDEAL project 118; programming period (2007–13) 113–14; Regional Policies and Funds 109

evaluation framework, participation initiatives 80–2; active participation 80–1, *85*; assessment 80–2; availability of communication tools 80–1; consultation 80–1, *85*; information factor 80–2, *85*; polls 80, *85*; weighting scheme 81–2, *81*

evaluation perspectives, LEX-IS project 20–9; context 21–2; outcomes 21, 26–9; process 21–4; system 21, 24–6

Evans-Crowley, J.; and Conroy, M. 104

Fishbein, M.; and Ajzen, I. 41
Fishkin, J. 1
Flores, F.; and Winogard, T. 124
Former Yugoslav Republic of Macedonia (FYROM) 8–9, 38
France 10; Poitou-Charentes Regional Government 10, 118–38
Freeman, R. 124
Frequently Asked Questions (FAQ) 62
Frewer, L.; and Rowe, G. 2–3

Garro, A.; and Ruffolo, M. 111
General Public Licence (GPL) 62
geographical information systems (GIS) 10; BLOG 99–114; e-approach for programming activities 104–9; knowledge organization and sharing 109–13; Marmo Platano-Melandro citizens (Italy) 97–115; participative and e-tools 97–115; programming documents and spatial information 100–9, **102–3**; WEBSITE 99–114; wikification 100, *see also* Territorial Integrated Projects; WEBGIS

Geological Survey (US) 100
Georgakopoulos, D.; *et al* 135
Geospatial free and Open Source Software (GFOSS) 106
Global Centre for ICT in Parliament (United Nations report) 13
good governance concept 59–60
Greece 8, 13–35, 77–96; Constitution 17; e-dialogos project 90–1; Information Society White Paper 83, 90; Parliament 13–35; Regions and prefectures 84–92, **86**, *see also* advanced information technologies; LEX-IS Project; regional/local level authority initiatives
gross domestic product (GDP) 94
Gruninger, M.; and Uschold, M. 110

Harvard strategic planning model 98
Heidegger, M. 61, 66–8, 75; three worlds 68
Held, D. 1; nine models of democracy 1
High Schools Preparatory Budget (Poitou-Charentes, France) 121

idea nodes 19
IDEAL-EU project 118–38; baseline conditions 120–8; Catalunya Regional Government (Spain) 118–38; contributions to e-participation 134–6; five analytical layers for scoping **119**; former participatory practices 120–1; frameworks 122; lessons learned from trials 131–4; Poitou-Charentes Regional Government (France) 118–38; policy process design, citizen participation 118–38; practitioner benefits 133–4; public decision-making process 122–4; summary and impact 121; three main steps 118–19; Toscana Regional Government (Italy) 118–38; Tulip 129–31, **129**, *see also* workflow model
information and communication technology (ICT) 4–6, 13, 31, 37, 65; acceptance determinant factors 41–2; accessibility/relevance/utility 5; decision support services 40; e-government tools and technologies 104–14; freeware platforms 113; infrastructure 137–8; Internet based platform 9–11, 32
Information Explosion Era 101
INSPIRE directive 105
institutional compatibility 65

INDEX

Inter-Parliamentary Union 13
interactive information tool 104; layers 106–7, *see also* WEBGIS
Internet 10; cafés 74; public access centre 91–2
interoperability 109–13; knowledge organization and sharing 109–13
ISO (19115) standard 106
Issue Based Information Systems (IBIS) 2, 14–18, 29, 32
Italy 8–10; e-participation tool construction and implementation 59–76; Emilia Romagna region 9, 59–76; first regional bill (Law No 69) 121; Marmo Platano-Melandro experience and achievements 10, 97–115; Minicipality of Modena 6, 67–73; Ministry for Technological Innovation 61–3; Toscana Regional Government 10, 118–38, *see also* geographical information systems

journalists 38–40, 50

Kalampokis, E.; *et al* 117
Kallikratis plan 83
Kitsuregawa, M.; *et al* 101
knowledge, sharing and organizing 109–13; lacking shared understanding framework 110
Koussouris, S.; *et al* 9, 37–58
Krimmer, R. 134

Lanzara, G. 63–4
Laurini, R.; and Murgante, B. 110
Legal Service of the Parliament (Greece) 30
LEX-IS Project 13–35; clarity of information and ease of understanding 22–6, **23–5**; and *Contracts of Voluntary Cohabitation* bill 18–20; contribution quality and satisfaction level 26–9, **27–8**; evaluation framework and methodology 19–22; Greek Parliament and public participation 13–35; perspectives and results (context/process/system/outcome) 22–9; quantitative evaluation questionnaire 33–5; structured e-forum and discussion tree 19–31, **19**; technical platform description 17–19; theoretical background 15–17; visualizations 19–24
local area network (LAN) 13
Loukis, E. 8, 13–35, 111; Macintosh, A. and Charalabidis, Y. 1–11

Macedonian Information Agency (MIA) 38, 48
Macintosh, A. 118, 122–3; Charalabidis, Y. and Loukis, E. 1–11; and Whyte, A. 4
Macpherson, L. 107–8

Members of Parliament (MPs) 13, 17, 32; assistants 27–8
Metadata National Repertory (CNIPA) 106
Minnesota strategic planning model 98
mobilization 74
Murgante, B.: *et al* 10, 97–115; and Laurini, R. 110

National Centre for ICT in the Public Administrations (CNIPA) 61–4
National News Agency of the Republic of Serbia (TANJUG) 38
neogeography 100
non-governmental organizations (NGOs) 9, 50–2

offline participation 19, 117
OGC standard 107
online tools and discussion formats 5–6
ontology 65–7, 110–13; concepts and entities 111; content/relation/actualization/enactment 65–72; domain 112; examples 111; PLANET 111–12; structural elements 110–11; super class structure 112, **113**; use in eParticipation research 65–7
Operational Programme for the Information Society (OPIS) 83
Organization for Economic Co-operation and Development (OECD) 2–4, 80; levels of participation 80

Panopoulou, E.; *et al* 9, 77–96
Paradigm of Urban Development 101
Partecipa.Net system 61–76; as assemblage 63–5; Base 62; Biblio 62; Forum 64–5, 68; *Forum Agorà* data 73; *gli orari della citta* case 67–73, 72; *per via Gallucci* case 67–72; Poll 62; project participation rate analysis 72–4, *see also* sense-making
participatory democracy concept 1
Pearson product-moment correlation coefficient 47, *49*
people-driven economy 99
Piaget, J. 66
plain vanilla concertation 120–1
policy process design 117–38, *see also* IDEAL-EU project
political clientelism 8
Political Evaluation Questionnaire 41, 44, 52; effects on User 56; impact on political life 56–7; results 48
Preparatory Action of the European Commission 14
Preparatory Action programmes 77
programming documents 100–9; and geographical information **102**; spatialization scheme **103**

INDEX

Public Administration processes 117–18, 132, 135, see also IDEAL-EU project
public authorities (PAs) 78, 83, 93–4; websites 78–80
public decision-making process 122–4; agenda setting 122; cycle and objectives 3–4; evaluation 123; five stages 122–3; policy creation 122–3; policy implementation and monitoring 123; prior analysis 122

question nodes 19

rational comprehensive planning approach 98
Regional Operational Programme (POR) 99, 103
regional/local level authority initiatives 77–96; comparison 87–90, **89**; discussion 92–4; e-dialogos project 90–1; evaluation framework 80–2, *81*; Information and Consultation factor 81; local level 82; Madrid Participa project 91–2; questionnaire and weighting scheme 80–2, *81*; results 84–92, *85*, *87–9*; score frequency **86**
Resca, A. 9, 59–76
reticular interactive planning approach 97–8
Rittel, H.; and Weber, M. 2, 15–16
Rowe, G.; and Frewer, L. 2–3
Royal Opera House (London) 99
Ruffolo, M.; and Garro, A. 111

Saebo, J.; et al 4
æbø, Ø 118
sense-making 67–76; atmosphere experienced by Users 71–2; and e-participation 67–76; meanings and interpretations 68–72; mediation style 68–9; participation characteristics 69–71; style of mediation 68–9
Serbia 8–9, 38; TANJUG 38
settlement node 24
single construct analyses and observations 45–6, **45**
Social Networking Platform (SNP) 119–33, 136–8; languages 128, see also IDEAL-EU
solidarity, sense of 73
Spain 8, 77–96; authority website scores *87*; Autonomous Communities and Provinces 84–92; Catalonia 10; Catalunya Regional Government 118–38; Constitution 84; Madrid Participa project 91–2, see also regional and local level authority initiatives
spatial information 100–9; data infrastructure 106
stakeholder groups 28; analysis 98, see also workflow model

stakeholder theory 124; discourse/reasoning/argument/negotiation 2; and problem 2
Staw, B.; and Sutton, R. 67
strategic planning 100–9; important aspects 98; rationality 102; spatial aspects 102–9; three families 97–8
strong democracy concept 1
super-classes, ontology 112; policy 112; project and plan 112; tools and actors 112
Sutton, R.; and Staw, B. 67
SWOT analysis 98
synthetic methodology 51

TAM factors and constructs 42–3; external factors 42–9, 55; intention to use 42–9, 55; perceived ease of use 42–9, 54; perceived usefulness 42–9, 54
Tambouris, E.; et al 118, 136
technology acceptability analysis 47–8, see also TAM
Technology Acceptance Model (TAM) 41–55, **43–4**; basic constructs 47–8; correlations (Pearson) 47, *49*; effect on User 48–50; factors/constructs 42–9, *45*, **45–7**; impact on political life 50–1; implementation 47–8; questionnaire and analysis 41–55; research hypotheses 43–4, *50*; system application 42–3
telecentres 74
Temporary Committee on Climate Change (EP) 119, 127
Territorial Integrated Projects (PITs) 99, 103–6; BLOG **108**; and the Marmo Platano-Melandro experience 97–115; WEBGIS architecture **106–7**
theory of reasoned action (TRA) 41
top-down planning approach 97–8; citizens engagement 4
trade unions 73
transparency 14
trust building actions 11
Twitter Dammerung (social opera) 99

u-City 101
United Kingdom 38
United Nations 13; three step enhancement plan 77
UNOX1 software application 61–4
Uschold, M.; and Gruninger, M. 110

Virtual Town Meeting (VTM) 119–31, 138
Visser, P.; and Bench-Capon, T. 112
visualizations 19–24, **21**, 30, 108; argument 14; political party **21**; technologies 30; and visioning 98–9, see also LEX-IS Project

INDEX

Web 2.0 social media 7, 101; for PTI 104–9; tools 10
Web Map Service (WMS) 105–7; tools (JPEG/GIF/PNG/URL) 107
Weber, M.; and Rittel, H. 2, 15–16
WEBGIS 100–14; architecture **106–7**; content groups 106–7; Marmo Platano-Melandro PIT **107**; user types 106
Weick, K. 66
Western Balkans Democracy Participation (WEB.DEP) 37–58, *see also* electronic participation pilot studies
Western Balkans National News Agency 38–40; e-Participation system 38–40; operational model 39–40, **40**; system overview 38
Westholm, H.; and Aichholzer, G. 117
Whyte, A.; and Macintosh, A. 4
wicked problems 14–17, 29
Wikinomics 98–9
Winogard, T.; and Flores, F. 124
Workflow Management Systems 137
workflow model, IDEAL-EU project 10, 120–31; characteristics 123; collaboration 124–6; decomposition 127, *127*; final and technical architecture 128–31; future instantiations *136*; initial 124–8, **126**; and the SNP importance 123–4; stages 126–7; stakeholders 124–8, *125*; the Tulip 129–31, **129**
World e-Parliament Report (2010) 13

XML standard 14

www.routledge.com/9780415448284

Related titles from Routledge

Euroscepticism in Southern Europe
A Diachronic Perspective

Edited by Susannah Verney

As a laboratory for the study of attitudes towards European integration, Southern Europe offers a particularly rich range of case studies, including a founder member (Italy), three 'second generation' states (Greece, Spain and Portugal), two recent entrants (Cyprus and Malta) and a negotiating candidate (Turkey). The volume traces the evolution of euroscepticism in each South European country, assessing its significance, identifying key turning-points and highlighting both continuity and change. Covering party and popular euroscepticism, the book illuminates similarities and differences between national experiences of euroscepticism.

This book was published as a special issue of *South European Society and Politics*.

Susannah Verney is Assistant Professor in European Integration at the University of Athens and has also held Visiting Fellowships at the Universities of Bristol and Bradford. She is Editor of *South European Society & Politics* (since 1999) and former Associate Editor of *The Journal of Modern Greek Studies* (2000-2002).

October 2011: 246 x 174: 224pp
Hb: 978-0-415-44828-4
£80 / $125

For more information and to order a copy visit
www.routledge.com/9780415448284

Available from all good bookshops

www.routledge.com/9780415459488

Related titles from Routledge

The Internet and European Parliamentary Democracy
A Comparative Study of the Ethics of Political Communication in the Digital Age
Edited by X. Dai and P. Norton

This book investigates the ethical challenges the internet presents to contemporary parliamentary democracy in Europe and how these challenges are being addressed. It fills an important gap in current literature, which until now has largely focused on the study of internet usage by politicians and institutions. There are widely differing views on whether parliamentary democracy will be strengthened or weakened in the information age.

The Internet and European Parliamentary Democracy compares four European parliaments: the British, European, Portuguese and Swedish Parliaments, using both quantitative methods (questionnaires and survey of websites) and qualitative methods (workshops and face-to-face interviews with parliamentarians and parliamentary staff).

This book was previously published as a special issue of the *Journal of Legislative Studies*.

July 2008: 156x234 168 pp.
Hb: 978-0-415-45948-8
£90/$133

For more information and to order a copy visit
www.routledge.com/ISBN 9780415459488

Available from all good bookshops